SAINT THOMAS AQUINAS

ON CHARITY
(DE CARITATE)

MEDIAEVAL PHILOSOPHICAL TEXTS IN TRANSLATION
NO. 10

MARQUETTE UNIVERSITY PRESS
1131 W. WISCONSIN AVENUE
MILWAUKEE 3, WISCONSIN

SAINT THOMAS AQUINAS, Saint.

ON CHARITY

(DE CARITATE)

Translated from the Latin
With an Introduction

By

Lottie H. Kendzierski, Ph. D.

Associate Professor of Philosophy, Marquette University

MARQUETTE UNIVERSITY PRESS, MILWAUKEE, WISCONSIN, 1960

Nihil Obstat:

Rev. John A. Schulien, S.T.D.
Censor Librorum

Imprimatur:

✠Gulielmus E. Cousins
Archiepiscopus Milwauchiensis
Milwauchiae, die 14 Martii, 1960

Second Printing 1971

INTRODUCTION

I.   The Works of St. Thomas Aquinas

St. Thomas Aquinas' career as a teacher and writer covered a period of more than twenty years (1252-1274). The writings of St. Thomas may be classified as theological works, commentaries, *Opuscula* or short treatises, and *Quaestiones Disputatae*. The following might be mentioned among the theological writings: the commentaries on the Gospels (1252-1254); the commentaries on the *Sentences* of Peter Lombard (1254-1256); the *Summa Contra Gentiles* (1260); the *Summa Theologiae* (1265-1272, which was left unfinished); the *Compendium Theologiae* (1272). The commentaries include those on Boethius, the *De Trinitate* and the *De Hebdomadibus* (1257-1258); on Dionysius, *De Divinis Nominibus* (about 1261); on the *Liber de Causis* (1268); on Aristotle, including parts of the *Organon*, the *Physics*, *On the Heavens*, *On Generation and Corruption*, *Metaphysics*, *On the Soul*, *Nicomachean Ethics*, *Politics* (1260-1272). Among the *Opuscula* or short treatises, some of the more prominent are the *De Ente et Essentia* (about 1252); *De Aeternitate Mundi; De Unitate Intellectus; De Substantiis Separatis* (the last three written during the years 1268-1272). The *Quaestiones Disputatae* (1256-1272) is comprised of eleven treatises, the lengthiest and perhaps most important being the *De Veritate* and the *De Potentia*.

Scholars have also grouped the works of St. Thomas according to three phases of his life. The first phase of St. Thomas' life is referred to as the first sojourn in Paris. This phase comprises two periods: the period of his baccalaureate (1252-1256); the period of his activity as Master at the University of Paris (1256-1259). The principal work composed during his baccalaureate was the *Commentary on the Sentences,* and the most developed writing as Master at the University of Paris (1256-1259) was the *Quaestiones Disputatae De Veritate*. The second phase of St. Thomas' life is called the sojourn in Italy (1259-1268). During this period St. Thomas wrote the *Summa Contra Gentiles* and some of the commentaries on the work of Aristotle. The *Summa Theologiae* dates from about 1265 to the time of his death. Parts of the *Quaestiones Disputatae* were written in Italy, namely, the *De Spiritualibus Creaturis*, the *De Potentia* and the *De Anima*. Finally, five *Quodlibeta* are also assigned to this Italian period. The third phase of St. Thomas' life is called the second sojourn in Paris (1268-1274). During this period St. Thomas wrote some commentaries

[1]

on Aristotle's works, the first six *Quodlibeta*, the *De Unitate Intellectus*, the *Liber de Causis*, commentaries on Scripture (*The Book of Job* and the *Gospel of St. John*), the *Compendium Theologiae*, the *De Substantiis Separatis* and the *Quaestiones Disputatae* (with the exception of the *De Veritate, De Potentia, De Spiritualibus Creaturis* and *De Anima*.[1]

II. Authenticity of the Disputed Questions

The *Disputed Questions* is a compilation of eleven distinct treatises or 510 disputations in the form of articles covering a variety of subject matter and a wealth of scholarly and penetrating analyses. The treatises are the following: the *De Veritate* (1256-1259), which contains twenty-nine questions and 253 disputations; the *De Potentia* (1265-1267), ten questions and 83 disputations; the *De Spiritualibus Creaturis* (1266-1272), one question and 11 disputations; the *De Anima* (after 1265), one question and 21 disputations; the *De Virtutibus in Communi* (1269-1272), one question and 13 disputations; the *De Caritate* (1269-1272), one question and 13 disputations; the *De Unione Verbi Incarnati* (1269-1272), one question and five disputations; the *De Malo* (1269-1272), sixteen questions and 101 disputations; the *De Virtutibus Cardinalibus* (1269-1272), one question and four disputations; the *De Spe* (1269-1272), one question and four disputations; the *De Correctione Fraterna* (1269-1272), one question and two disputations.

Much literature has been written on the authenticity, date and style of the *Disputed Questions*.[2] Various introductions to the *Disputed Questions*, along with introductions to individual questions, have adequately developed these points.[3]

---

[1] On the chronology and authenticity of the works of St. Thomas, see P. Mandonnet, *Des écrits authentiques de s. Thomas* (2 ed.; Fribourg: 1910); P. Synave, "Le catalogue officiel des oeuvres de s. Thomas d'Aquin," *Archives* III, (1928); M. Grabmann, *Die Werke des hl. Thomas von Aquin, Beiträge* XXII, No. 1-2, (Münster: 1931); J. Destrez, *Études critique sur les oeuvres de s. Thomas d'Aquin, Bibliothique Thomiste* (Paris: 1933) XVII; A. Walz, "Saint Thomas d'Aquin. Écrits," in *Dictionnaire de théologie Catholique*, XV, No. 1, (1926), pp. 635-641; M. D. Chenu, *Introduction à l'étude de saint Thomas d'Aquin*, XI; (Montreal: Institut l'Étude Médiévaux 1950), XI; I. T. Eschmann, "A Catalogue of St. Thomas' Works," in *The Christian Philosophy of St. Thomas Aquinas* (New York: Random House, 1956), pp. 381-430.

[2] On the authenticity of the *Disputed Questions*, see P. Mandonnet, "Chronologie des Questions Disputées de saint Thomas d'Aquin," *Revue Thomiste*, (1918); P. Synave, "Le problème chronologique des Questions Disputées de s. Thomas d'Aquin," *Revue Thomiste*, (1926); J. Koch, *Ueber die Reihenfolge der Questiones Disputatae des hl. Thomas von Aquin*, in *Philosophische Jahrbuch*, XXXVII, (1924), 359-367; P. Glorieux, "Les Questions Disputées de S. Thomas et leur suite chronologie," *Recherches de théologie ancienne et médiévale*, (1932), pp. 5-33; M. D. Chenu, *op. cit.*, pp. 67-77, 241-245.

[3] The reader will find the following introductions helpful. P. M. Pession, "Introductio Generalis," *Quaestiones disputatae S. Thomae* (Turin: 1949), I, vii-xxi;

The *Disputed Question on Charity* was written late in St. Thomas' life. The date usually preferred is 1269-1272.[4] No critical edition of this text is available at the present time; the Leonine editors have advised that this text will be completed in about ten years. In the meantime, it is hoped that this English translation will serve some purpose to the English reader. The Marietti edition (*Quaestiones Disputatae*, Turin, 1949, Vol. II) is the basis for this translation, and instances of a corrupt text have been indicated. Scriptural references are translations from the Latin Vulgate; at times references to Aristotle and other authorities have had to be changed.

III. *The Style of the* Quaestiones Disputatae. *Comparison of the* Quaestiones Disputatae *with the* Quaestiones Quodlibetales *and the* Summa Theologiae.

In mediaeval theological instruction, the *quaestio* method began during the exercises in disputation which the master prepared for his pupils.[5] The most important in subject matter and the most frequent were the *Disputationes Ordinariae.* Every master held them several times a year, and these were closely connected with his lectures. The characteristic feature of the *Disputationes Ordinariae* is the weighty, difficult, and related themes, often representing a large and uniform complexity of questions, which were discussed with all the thoroughness and depth of scholastic research. On such a comprehensive subject, many *Disputationes Ordinariae* could be arranged, sometimes extending over a period of several years.

The procedure of a single disputation, which lasted for two days, was

L. W. Keeler, *Sancti Thomae Aquinatis, Tractatus de Spiritualibus Creaturis* (Rome: University Gregoriana, 1938); M. Fitzpatrick and J. Wellmuth, *On Spiritual Creatures* (Milwaukee: Marquette University Press, 1949), pp. 3-11; J. P. Reid, *On the Virtues (in General)* (Providence: College Press, 1951), pp. ix-xxvii; V. J. Bourke, "Introduction to St. Thomas on Truth," in *Truth* (Chicago: Henry Regnery Co., 1952), I, xiii-xxvi.

4 See P. Synave, "Le problème chronologique des Questions Disputées de s. Thomas d'Aquin," *op. cit.*, pp. 155-158; M. Grabmann, *op. cit.*, p. 307; M. D. Chenu, *op. cit.*, p. 242. The date given by P. Glorieux is 1269-1270, *op. cit.*, p. 31. The date given by P. Mandonnet is 1270-1272, "Chronologie des Questions Disputées de saint Thomas d'Aquin," *op. cit.*, pp. 16, 266-287, 341-371. The date given by F. Van Steenberghen is 1271-1272, *Siger dans l'histoire d'Aristotelisme* (Louvain: 1942), pp. 541 ff.

5 On the style of the *Disputed Questions*, see M. D. Chenu, *op. cit.*, pp. 67-77. On the history of this style, see G. Paré, A. Brunet, and P. Tremblay, *La Renaissance du XII$_e$ siècle. Les écoles et l'enseignement* (Ottawa: Institute d'Études Médiévale d'Ottawa III, 1933), pp. 128-132; M. D. Chenu, "Un essai de methode theologique aux XII$_e$ siècle," *Revue des Sciences Philosophique et Theologique*, (Paris: Librarie Philosophique: J. Vrin, 1935), pp. 258-267.

[3]

the following. On the first day, the master presided, with the student called upon to answer the arguments and difficulties raised by the master on the proposed question. Students and scholars were present at this solemn academic function. On the second day, the teacher took the active part. He put in order and grouped the arguments and objections which were brought up on the preceding day of disputation. He then advanced against these objections a *sed contra* or short argument, drawn from reason and authority, which in a general way announced his solution of the problem. The master then undertook his independent solution of the question in a detailed and thorough fashion by entering into the historical and speculative connections and presuppositions, formulating his own definitive answer and substantiating it. This decision of the question by the master was termed the *Determinatio Magistralis.* On the basis of this decision, the master finally disposed of the objections against it. The completed *Disputationes Ordinariae* became the *Quaestiones Disputatae.*

The *Quaestiones Disputatae* differ from the *Quaestiones Quodlibetales* in that the latter were held twice a year, usually during Advent and during Lent. The *Quaestiones Quodlibetales* dealt with diverse and unrelated questions and did not enter too deeply into the problems. They were frequently arranged in a loose and superficial order under the direction of the master.

There is an intimate relation between the *Quaestiones Disputatae* and the *Summa Theologiae.* The style of the disputation is similar to the article form of the *Summa,* beginning with a statement of the question, followed by a series of difficulties, the *on the contrary,* the main answer or reply and, finally, the answers or replies to the objections. The questions in the *Quaestiones Disputatae* include more difficulties than those of the *Summa;* they sometimes contain a statement of the difficulty (*sed dicebat . . .*) followed immediately by a special argument to the contrary (*sed contra . . .*). Whereas the *Summa* has one *sed contra,* the *Quaestiones Disputatae* offer more arguments to the contrary. It is common to find in the *Quaestiones Disputatae,* following the replies to the difficulties, a series of answers to the arguments *sed contra.* These arguments to the contrary are not necessarily the thought of St. Thomas but are rather statements in opposition to the difficulties.

In addition to the similarity in style of the *Quaestiones Disputatae* and the *Summa Theologiae,* the subjects of discussion are almost identical. For example, the *Disputed Question on Truth,* which preceded the *Summa* by almost ten years, deals with questions that are found in the three parts of the *Summa.* The other *Disputed Questions* were, for the most part, written along with some parts of the *Summa* and resemble the *Summa* in content.

[4]

The outstanding characteristics of the *Disputed Questions* are their depth and fullness of detail. Inasmuch as the material exposed in the arguments and counter-arguments (*sed contra*) grew directly out of disputations, the *Disputed Questions* display a richer content than was compatible with the purpose of the *Summa*. And because the arguments or objections issued from the circle of University professors and students, the *Disputed Questions* show more clearly than any other writing the convergence of Thomistic doctrine with the theology of the age. The historical and critical reviews of traditional opinions and attempted solutions are searchingly made and the body of the article is, as a rule, quite detailed and penetrating. The formulation of the *Determinatio Magistralis* and the finished product, or the *Quaestiones Disputatae*, under the critical inspection of the entire faculty called for an exceptionally precise elaboration of ideas and distinctions.[6]

In this way, the *Disputed Questions* and the *Summa Theologiae* were written for different purposes. Whereas the *Disputed Questions* were intended for the proficient, the *Summa*, as St. Thomas states in the Prologue, ought not only to instruct the proficient, but should instruct beginners. St. Thomas' purpose in the *Summa* was to treat of the things which belong to the Christian religion in such a way that it is compatible with the instruction of beginners. In the Prologue, St. Thomas mentions three faults in the method and purpose of instructing beginners. (1) Beginners have been hampered partly because of the multiplication of useless questions, articles, and arguments. Simplicity, clearness, and strict objectivity were to be the basic qualities of the method proper to the *Summa*. (2) Beginners have been hampered by the lack of systematic arrangement and sequence. The Prologue specifies that this drawback to the progress of theology students consisted in the fact that the subjects of knowledge necessary for the beginner were not taught according to the order of the subject matter. The subjects were not presented in a methodical and systematic sequence, but followed the order suggested by the exposition demanded in books, or as the occasion for disputation arose. The disputation method, therefore, was not adapted to the didactic needs of the students of Sacred Doctrine. (3) Beginners were hampered by the frequent and futile repetition of the same topics in the oral teaching and in the writings of the scholastics which engendered weariness and confusion in the minds of listeners and readers.[7] St. Thomas sought to retain the greatest amount of clearness and precision; he assigned to every subject its logical place and thus avoided tiresome repetitions.

[6] See M. D. Chenu, *Introduction à l'étude de saint Thomas d'Aquin,* p. 65.
[7] See the Prologue to the *Summa Theologiae* in *Basic Writings of St. Thomas Aquinas,* ed. A. C. Pegis (New York: Random House, 1945), Vol. I.

Further, St. Thomas introduced new articles into his lectures, adopted a new and clear method of scientific research and synthesis, and developed new proofs in his demonstration.

IV. Doctrinal Summary

It was stated above[8] that the subjects treated in the *Disputed Questions* and in the *Summa* were the same. This is especially true of the *Disputed Question on Charity*. St. Thomas discusses the virtue of charity at great length in the *Summa,* and devotes six questions and sixty-nine articles to the virtue of charity.[9] St. Thomas' arguments are essentially the same in both works.

In the *Summa,* St. Thomas treats charity according to the following headings: (1) charity in itself;[10] (2) the subject of charity;[11] (3) the object of charity;[12] (4) the order of charity;[13] (5) the principal act of charity,[14] and (6) the precepts of charity.[15] The same points are treated in the *Disputed Question on Charity* but with slight variations.

The starting point, both in the *Summa* and in the *Disputed Question on Charity,* is the consideration of charity in itself.[16] In Article I of the *Disputed Question on Charity,* St. Thomas begins by saying that charity is either something created in the human soul, or it is the Holy Spirit.[17] St. Thomas' argument is largely a refutation and exposition of Peter Lombard's text which identifies charity with the Holy Spirit. Now if charity is the Holy Spirit, then the act of charity in man cannot be voluntary or meritorious, for man would be an agent only instrumentally. And there appears to be a contradiction: charity must be something created in the human soul; yet charity exceeds the capacity of human nature. St. Thomas' resolution of the difficulty is made in the following way. In order that the act of charity be voluntary, some habit must be added to human nature, perfecting the will in such a way that the action would proceed from an intrinsic principle. The Holy Spirit, therefore, moves man's will to the act of love by giving the form and power whereby the will is inclined to that which He Himself moves it, so that the will tends to the act of love of its own free accord.

---

[8] See p. 4.
[9] *Summa Theologiae* II-II, qq. 23-27, 44.
[10] *Sum. Theol.* II-II, q. 23, aa. 1-8. See *Quaestiones disputatae: De caritate* aa. 1-5.
[11] *Sum. Theol.* II-II, q. 24, aa. 1-12. See *De caritate* aa. 6, 12, 13.
[12] *Sum. Theol.* II-II, q. 25, aa. 1-12. See *De caritate* aa. 7, 8.
[13] *Sum. Theol.* II-II, q. 26, aa. 1-13. See *De caritate* a. 9.
[14] *Sum. Theol.* II-II, q. 27, aa. 1-8. See *De caritate* a. 10.
[15] *Sum. Theol.* II-II, q. 44, aa. 1-8. See *De caritate* a. 11.
[16] *Sum. Theol.* II-II, q. 23, aa. 1-8. See *De caritate* aa. 1-5.
[17] See *Sum. Theol.* II-II, q. 23, a. 2; *Scripta super libros Sententiarum* I d. 17, q. 1, a. 1.

Charity is, therefore, a habit created in the human soul. Article II is an attempt to establish this habit as a virtue.[18] There are some reasons why it would seem that there is no need for the virtue of charity: (1) charity is included in the other virtues; (2) grace is adequate to unite man to God, and (3) if charity is friendship, and if friendship implies equality, there can be no friendship or equality between man and God.[19] The necessity for saying that charity is a virtue is posited in this way. Virtue is that which makes man good and renders his work good. Virtue, therefore, operates for the good; and virtue operates well for the good, viz., voluntarily, readily, with delight, and firmly. Now some goods are by nature in the human will, e.g., the love of the good of reason. However, there are other goods which are not in man by nature, for example, the artistic good, the political good, and the highest good. The love of the highest good, as the object of beatitude, requires infused virtue. In this way charity is not only a virtue, but is the most powerful of the virtues.

Charity is not only the most powerful of the virtues, but charity is the form of the virtues.[20] The objections, in the main, center around the notion that charity cannot be the form of other virtues because form confers being. Charity, however, does not give being to the other virtues. Nor is charity included in the definition of the other virtues, for then all the virtues would be of one species. St. Thomas' answer is that each virtue has a common or general form from charity. Charity, therefore, gives a common species to each virtue and is the form of the virtues as informing the other virtues; charity is not part of the essence of the other virtues. The acts of all the other virtues are ordered to the proper end of charity which is its object, namely, the highest good. Therefore, in the acts of all the virtues, there is the formal element which comes from charity; and charity is the form of all the virtues because all the acts of the virtues are ordered to the highest good, which is the end of charity. In this way, charity commands the acts of the virtues and is called the mother and root of the virtues because, from its end, it produces the acts of all the virtues.

Though the form of the other virtues, charity is nevertheless a virtue in itself, distinct from the other virtues. Article IV will establish charity as one virtue.[21] Now it would appear that because acts are distinguished

---

[18] The same subject is treated in *Sum. Theol.* II-II, q. 23, a. 3; *In III Sent.* d. 27, q. 2, a. 2.

[19] St. Thomas devotes a special article on charity as friendship in *Sum. Theol.* II-II, q. 23, a. 1.

[20] *De caritate* a. 3. On charity as the form of the virtues, see *Sum. Theol.* II-II, q. 23, a. 8; *In II Sent.* d. 26, q. 1, a. 4, ad 5m, *In III Sent.* d. 23, q. 3, a. 1; d. 27, q. 2, a. 4, qa. 3; *Quaestiones disputatae: De veritate* q. 14, a. 5; *Quaestiones disputatae: De malo* q. 7, a. 2.

[21] *De caritate*, a. 4. See *Sum. Theol.* II-II, q. 23, a. 5; *In III Sent.* d. 27, q. 2, a. 4, qa. 1. In the *Summa*, St. Thomas first discusses charity as a special virtue (II-II,

[7]

by their objects, and since charity has two objects, viz., God and neighbor, therefore charity is two virtues. St. Thomas argues that charity regards God as the principal object, and neighbor is loved because of God. Materially, therefore, there are two objects in charity; formally, however, they are considered as one object. Further, though two precepts are given in charity, viz., *Love the Lord thy God* and *Love thy neighbor,* these precepts concern the acts of the virtues; and it does not follow that from a diversity of precepts, there is a diversity of virtues.

St. Thomas' analysis of the unity of virtue is made in the following way. The unity of any power or habit is derived from the object. In the object, the form is that according to which the object is referred to a power or a habit; the matter is that in which it has its foundation. Power or habit, therefore, are related essentially to the formal notion of the object, and only accidentally to the material notion of the object. This distinction can be carried over to the virtue of charity, where man can love something in a twofold way. First, by reason of its very self, and secondly, by reason of another. If someone is loved for his own sake, his family, relatives, and friends are loved inasmuch as they are related to the one loved. However, in all of these, there is only one formal notion of love, viz., the good of the one loved for his own sake. In this way, charity loves God for His own sake; and because of Him, it loves all others according as they are ordered to God. There is, therefore, one virtue by which God and neighbor are loved.

The last point that St. Thomas makes regarding the virtue of charity considered in itself, is charity considered as a special virtue.[22] It would seem that charity is not a special virtue because it is included in the definition of each virtue and operates in the acts of the other virtues. St. Thomas argues that charity has God as its formal object, whereas the other virtues have God as their final end; thus the definition of charity is other than the definition of the other virtues. Nor does charity elicit the acts of the other virtues; charity commands the acts of the virtues because they are related to the end of charity. Charity is also a special virtue because its object is not a common good or the good in general, but the highest good; thus charity is not a general virtue, but is the highest virtue.[23]

Though charity is spoken of as existing in different subjects, viz., in the mind, in the soul, in the heart, and in strength, nevertheless charity

q. 23, a. 4), and then charity as one virtue (II-II, q. 23, a. 5). On the other hand, in the *De caritate,* St. Thomas first discusses charity as one virtue (a. 4), and then charity as a special virtue (a. 5).

[22] *De caritate* a. 5. See *Sum. Theol.* II-II, q. 23, a. 4; *In III Sent.* d. 27, q. 2, a. 4, qa. 2; *De malo* q. 8, a. 2; q. 9, a. 2.

[23] St. Thomas devotes a special article to charity as the highest virtue. See *Sum. Theol.* II-II, q. 23, a. 6.

exists only in the will which moves the other powers through its command. And through its manner of commanding the other virtues, charity can even take away all sins; however, the other virtues are necessary to directly and in an elicited way drive out sin. Finally, all the virtues are generated and corrupted with charity. Charity is generated along with the other virtues, not because it is not distinct from the other virtues, but because the works of God are perfect. Thus, when charity is established, so all the other virtues are established which are necessary for salvation. Charity, however, is corrupted with the other virtues because whatever is opposed to the other virtues, is opposed to charity. The conclusion on this point is that since man is disposed through charity to regard himself well toward his final end, it is necessary to have other virtues by which he will be well-disposed toward the means to the end.[24]

St. Thomas then turns to the subject of charity. Three articles of the *Disputed Question on Charity* are devoted to this point;[25] in the *Summa* there are twelve articles.[26] The articles in the *Summa* deal largely with the following: the will as the subject of charity, charity as an infused virtue, the reception of charity, the increase of charity, the perfection and the grades of charity, the decrease of charity, the loss of charity,[27] and the loss of charity through mortal sin.[28] These subjects are included in the three articles of the *Disputed Question on Charity*, and, in part, in the first five articles.

In Article VI, St. Thomas asks whether charity can exist with mortal sin. His reasons for a negative answer can be summarized briefly. (1) Though charity is stronger than moral virtue, the habit of charity is taken away through one act of vice, whereas one act of vice does not take away moral virtue. But since moral virtue is acquired by acts, and is an inclination of power to act, this inclination is not entirely taken away by sin. The influence that God exerts in the operation of charity, however, is taken away by one act. (2) Charity is strongest, whereas sin is weakest because evil is wicked and infirm. Thus it would seem that mortal sin cannot drive out charity. St. Thomas answers by saying that sin does not drive out charity by its own power, but only in virtue of the fact that man voluntarily subjects himself to sin. (3) There is no contrary to the pleasure which comes from contemplating God; therefore there is no contrary to charity,

<hr>

[24] This completes St. Thomas' treatment of the virtue of charity considered in itself, as discussed in the first five articles of the *De caritate*. In the *Summa*, there are three more articles, treating of charity as friendship, charity as the most excellent of the virtues, and whether any virtue is possible without charity. These three points have been incorporated in the first five articles of the *De caritate*.

[25] *De caritate* a. 6, 12, 13.

[26] *Sum. Theol.* II-II, q. 24, aa. 1-12.

[27] *De caritate* a. 11.

[28] *De caritate* aa. 6, 13.

and thus charity cannot be driven out by sin. St. Thomas' solution is that the love of God is contrary to the love of sin, which excludes man from God. Contemplation, in so far as there is no contrary, is not an act elicited by charity; charity is only commanded by it as its effect. (4) Just as faith and hope exist without form, it would seem that charity can exist without form. Charity, however, cannot exist without form because charity has God as its formal object. Faith and hope, on the other hand, have God as their final end; thus they can exist without form for they are not the form of the other virtues. (5) Contraries are of the same genus; but sin is an act whereas charity is a habit. Therefore it would seem that sin is not contrary to charity. St. Thomas argues that acts are indirectly contrary to habits according as they conform to contrary habits, e.g., similar acts are generated from similar habits, and similar acts cause similar habits, though not all habits are caused by acts.

Having answered the difficulties, St. Thomas clearly summarizes his position. The Holy Spirit dwells in man as long as he has charity; but charity is driven out when sin enters and cannot exist along with sin. Nor can one be worthy of eternal life and eternal punishment at the same time. Mortal sin, therefore, consists in choosing something other than to live according to God and to inhere in that other; by this fact one loves some other good more than he loves God. Since charity is infused in man by God not only in the beginning, but also in its entire duration, when mortal sin enters, it obstructs the direct sight of the soul for God; and the flow of charity is stopped. The soul of man can again return to God and charity, with the help of divine grace, by regarding God rightly, and by loving Him above all things.

The object of charity follows the discussion of the nature of charity as a virtue, and the subject of charity. In the *Summa*, St. Thomas treats the object of charity in twelve articles,[29] listing some possible objects to be loved out of charity: God, neighbor, irrational creatures, self, body, sinners, enemies, angels, and demons. Two articles in the *Disputed Question on Charity* are devoted to a discussion of the above objects as possible objects of the virtue of charity.[30]

St. Thomas asks whether a rational nature can be the object to be loved out of charity.[31] First, all things should be loved out of charity, by ordering them to those who have a capacity for beatitude; not, however, by wishing beatitude for them. Secondly, angels and God, though not known by man in themselves, are to be loved; however, man is not able to love God here with the perfection with which he will love Him in heaven, through the

---

[29] *Sum. Theol.* II-II, q. 25, aa. 1-12.
[30] *De caritate* aa. 7, 8.
[31] *De caritate* a. 7. See *Sum. Theol.* II-II, q. 25, a. 3; *In III Sent.* d. 28, q. 1, a. 2.

direct vision of His essence. Angels, on the other hand, should be loved because man is able to share with the angels in the life of glory. Thirdly, a difficulty arises with regard to love of self and love of neighbor. Love of self is usually looked upon as a vice, and the precepts of charity seem to apply only to.the love of God and the love of neighbor. St. Thomas explains the precepts of charity by saying that in the precept of loving God and neighbor, there is included the precept that man love himself; for it is said, *Love thy neighbor as thyself*. Thus, man is induced to love God, by which he especially loves himself and wishes for himself the highest good; and in this love of self there is included the love of the body.

The object to be loved out of charity is summarized by St. Thomas according to a twofold consideration: (1) one for whom we wish the good; and (2) the good which we wish for someone. (1) Only intellectual nature ought to be loved out of charity since only such a nature can enjoy the good of divine beatitude. Now some objects are able to have eternal beatitude of different kinds; therefore four objects are distinguished to be loved out of charity. (a) God has eternal beatitude through His own essence; and intellectual nature has eternal beatitude through participation. God ought to be loved out of charity as the root of beatitude. (b) Every man ought to love himself according as he participates in beatitude. (c) Neighbor ought to be loved as an associate in the participation of beatitude. (d) The body should be loved according as beatitude redounds to it.

(2) According to the good we wish for others, everything can be loved out of charity insofar as these are certain goods of those who are able to enjoy beatitude. In this way, all creatures are a means for man to tend towards beatitude, and all creatures are ordered to the glory of God inasmuch as the divine goodness is manifested in them. Thus, the love of charity includes all human loves, with the exception of those based on sin, which cannot be ordered to beatitude.

In the *Disputed Question on Charity*, St. Thomas devotes a special article on the love of enemies as an object of charity;[32] and asks, more specifically, if the love of enemies arises from the perfection of a counsel. The precepts of the Old Law command not.only that the affection of love be had for enemies, i.e., love your enemies; but also that the effect of love must be imparted to them, i.e., do good to those who hate you. The love of enemies is, however, contrary to the inclination of nature. Charity, therefore, perfects the natural inclination of man and loves in man what is of God; it hates sin, which is not of God. Further, if the sign that a habit is formed is pleasure in the work, then to love a friend is more pleasing than to love an enemy. However, though to love an enemy as enemy

[32] *De caritate* a. 8. See *Sum. Theol.* II-II, q. 25, aa. 8-9; *In III Sent.* d. 30, q. 1, a. 1; *De Perfectione Vitae Spiritualis* c. 14; *Ad Romanos* c. 12, l. 13.

is difficult and even impossible; to love an enemy because of the love of God, this love makes easy that which seems impossible in itself.

The love of enemies, therefore, comes under the necessity of a precept in one way; and in another way, it comes under the perfection of a counsel. The love of God must predominate over the love of any other thing, and even over the hatred of the contrary of that thing. Thus it is from the necessity of a precept that enemies be loved. On the other hand, man is bound in affection and in effect to love all and to pray for all, even those not united to him by a special bond. When man shows a special affection and effect of love to those who are joined to him for the sake of God, this is perfect charity and follows from a counsel. Charity is the more perfect according to which man is moved to love and to do good, not only to those who are near, but also to those who are far away and even enemies, both in a general and in a special way.

The order of charity is discussed in Article IX.[33] The *Summa* devotes thirteen articles to this problem,[34] and they are primarily concerned with the following: (1) should God be loved more than neighbor and self; (2) should man love himself and his own body more than his neighbor; (3) should one neighbor be loved more than another; (4) should those who are united be loved more than others; (5) should mother be loved more than father, wife more than mother and father, benefactor or those who have been benefitted, and (6) does the order of charity remain in heaven.

These same points are discussed in Article IX of the *Disputed Question on Charity*. St. Thomas summarizes the order of charity in the following way. First, God should be loved above all things, both in affection and in the effect of love. Secondly, man should love himself. Thirdly, man should love his neighbor. Among his neighbors, man ought to give mutual help to those who are more closely united or related to him. Thus, in affection, one neighbor ought to be loved more than another; and he is loved out of charity which commands the act of the other lawful friendships. Fourthly, man ought to love his body. Regarding the charity of heaven, however, there is no order because those who are in heaven are united to their final end, and their love is regulated solely by that end. There is order in heaven only as regards one's nearness to God, and therefore those who are closer to God are loved more.

In Article X, St. Thomas returns to the subject he started with, namely, the nature of the virtue of charity, and more especially to an analysis of

---

[33] See *Sum. Theol.* II-II, q. 26, a. 1; *In III Sent.* d. 29, q. 1, a. 1.
[34] *Sum. Theol.* II-II, q. 26, aa. 1-13.

the perfection of the charity of this life.[35] In the *Summa,* on the other hand, the order is somewhat different. After discussing the order of charity, St. Thomas discusses the principal act of charity, i.e., to love.[36] No article in the *Disputed Question on Charity* specifically discusses the act of charity; the act of charity is, however, treated throughout the other articles.[37]

The analysis of the perfection of charity in this life is introduced by the precept in which man is bound to love God with his whole heart, which does not mean that man should do this; but rather that man should tend toward this, for man's soul cannot be always directed perfectly to God in knowledge and in love in this life. God can be loved wholly by man in this life only insofar as there is nothing in man's affection contrary to the divine love. Further, the charity of this life cannot be perfect because the object of charity exceeds the powers of man. Moreover, for charity to be perfect, man would have to be entirely free from sin, which is not possible in this life.

St. Thomas says that the perfect is spoken of in three ways. (1) The perfect in itself which lacks no perfection, and is said only of God. (2) The perfect according to nature which lacks nothing of what it should possess by nature. Man is impeded in this life to loving God as much as he is able because of (a) the contrary inclination of the soul; (b) the occupation with worldly affairs, (c) the infirmity of this life, and the burden of the body.[38] In this life, it is possible for man to live without (a) and (b), but not (c); and therefore charity can be perfect in this life according to the first two ways, but not according to the third. Finally, (3) the perfect according to time lacks nothing of the things which it is created to have

---

[35] See *Sum. Theol.* II-II, q. 24, aa. 8; q. 184, a. 2; *In III Sent.* d. 27, q. 3, a. 4; *De Perf. Vitae Spir.* c. 3; *Ad Philippios* c. 3.

[36] *Sum. Theol.* II-II, q. 27, aa. 1-8.

[37] The act of charity, for example, in *Sum. Theol.* II-II, q. 27, aa. 1-8, includes an analysis of the following points: (1) whether it is more proper to charity to love or to be loved; (2) whether love is benevolence; (3) whether God is loved in Himself out of charity; (4) whether God can be loved wholly and immediately in this life; (5) whether charity has any measure; and (6) whether it is more meritorious to love enemy rather than friend; or to love God more than neighbor.

[38] St. Thomas has shown the manner in which man should love himself and his body; and therefore it might appear strange at this point to speak of the "burden of the body" as an impediment to the perfection of the charity of this life. It is beyond the purpose of this text to elaborate on St. Thomas' position on the unity of man and the relation of the soul to the body. It would seem that when St. Thomas speaks of the burden of the body, he is following St. Augustine very closely. It might also be noted that apart from the authority of Aristotle on philosophical matters, St. Augustine is, for St. Thomas, the authority on theological matters. One has only to read the works of St. Augustine to find the penetrating and exhaustive emphasis on charity; it is no wonder, therefore, that St. Thomas finds St. Augustine so appealing when he himself undertakes to explain the virtue of charity.

according to a particular time; and therefore perfect charity according to time can be had by man in this life.

St. Thomas then asks if all are bound to perfect charity[39] and argues that it is not possible to refer all acts to God in this life, just as it is not possible to know God in this life. However, all things can be referred to God by virtue, and this pertains to the perfection of charity to which all are bound. First of all, men are bound to the perfection of charity which follows from the species of charity, and this consists in removing any inclination toward the contrary of charity. Secondly, men are not bound to the perfection of charity which pertains to the well-being of charity, and which consists in the taking away of the occupations of the world by which human affection is hindered from freely advancing to God. Thirdly, men are not bound to the perfection of charity which is not possible in this life because of the infirmity of this life and the burden of the body. Finally, men are not bound to the perfection of charity which no created nature can attain, for the perfect in itself is said of God alone.

The last two articles of the *Disputed Question on Charity* concern the loss of charity. In Article XII, St. Thomas asks whether charity, once possessed, can be lost.[46] In sum, charity, according to its own power, cannot be lost; but it can be lost because of the power of the changing choice of the subject when he resists the movement of the Holy Spirit.

This conclusion is arrived through a fourfold consideration of charity. (1) On the part of the Holy Spirit moving the soul to the love of God and neighbor. Here the movement of the Holy Spirit is always efficacious according to its own intention. Therefore, in those to whom the Holy Spirit freely wishes to give a persevering movement of divine love sin cannot drive out charity, although charity can be driven out on the part of the freedom of the will in man. Thus, the Holy Spirit freely gives to some that at times they might be moved to the love of God, but He does not give in such a way that they might persevere to the end in that love. (2) According to the power of charity. Here no one can sin by virtue of that charity. (3) According to the will, insofar as charity is subject to the will. In this life, charity does not perfect all the powers of the soul and is not always perfectly directed to God; therefore the charity in this life can be lost on the part of the subject. (4) Charity on the part of the subject ac-

---

[39] *De caritate* a. 11. See *In III Sent.* d. 29, q. 1, a. 8, qa. 2. There is no specific treatment of this point in the *Summa*. However, St. Thomas discusses the precept of charity at great length in *Sum. Theol.* II-II, q. 44, aa. 1-8, and this terminates his discussion of charity in the *Summa*. On the other hand, in the last two articles of the *De caritate* (aa. 12-13), St. Thomas returns to a discussion of the nature of the virtue of charity and asks whether charity can be lost once it is possessed; and whether charity can be lost through one act of mortal sin.

[40] See *Sum. Theol.* II-II, q. 24, a. 11, where this is discussed under the nature of charity. See also *Ad Rom.* VIII, 7; *Ad Corinthios* XIII, 3.

cording as it is compared in a special way to charity itself, as potency is compared to habit. The habit of virtue inclines man to act rightly, and through it man has the right estimation of the end. Yet one who has the habit of virtue sometimes acts contrary to the inclination of his proper habit; for a thing seems to him to be something else according to some other mode, such as passion which leads him away from the correct estimation. Only in heaven, therefore, is one unable to act contrary to the habit of charity because no one is able to have any judgment about the end and the object of charity other than that which he has according to the inclination of charity; and thus, only the charity of heaven cannot be lost. In this life, however, the soul does not see the essence of divine goodness but only some of its effects, which can seem either good or not-good according to different considerations, e.g., the spiritual good does not seem good insofar as it is contrary to some bodily pleasure.

St. Thomas has shown the way in which the charity of this life can be lost. He will then show that charity can be lost through one act of mortal sin, and this is the subject of the last article of this Question.[41] Charity is lost in two ways: directly, through an actual contempt of God; and indirectly, e.g., one who is not thinking of God consents to something against the law of God because of some passion of fear or concupiscence, and thus loses charity. St. Thomas cites the loss of charity in the denial of Peter as an indirect loss, caused by fear rather than a deliberate will. Since the habit of charity cannot exist along with mortal sin, the habit of charity is lost through one act of mortal sin. For, the habit of charity does not have a cause in the subject, but depends entirely on an extrinsic cause, viz., the Holy Spirit. Therefore God is the cause of charity and of grace in the soul both in their becoming and in their preservation; thus the habit of charity immediately ceases when the soul turns itself away from God through sin.

The translator would like to thank Fr. Gerard Smith, S.J., and Fr. Francis C. Wade, S.J., for their kind encouragement in the preparation of this text. Thanks is also due to Fr. Wade, Dr. James H. Robb and Dr. Paul M. Byrne for their careful examination of the manuscript and for many helpful criticisms and suggestions. To Miss Astrid Richie, whose assistance in this work was invaluable, I am also grateful.

LOTTIE H. KENDZIERSKI

---

[41] *De caritate* a. 13. See *De caritate* a. 6; *Sum. Theol.* II-II, q. 24, a. 12; *In III Sent.* d. 31, q. 1, a. 1.

[15]

DISPUTED QUESTION ON CHARITY

The first point of inquiry is whether charity is something created in the soul, or is it the Holy Spirit Itself?

2. Whether charity is a virtue?
3. Whether charity is the form of the virtues?
4. Whether charity is one virtue?
5. Whether charity is a special virtue?
6. Whether there can be charity with mortal sin?
7. Whether the object to be loved out of charity is a rational nature?
8. Whether loving one's enemies comes from the perfection of a counsel?
9. Whether there is some order in charity?
10. Whether charity can be perfect in this life?
11. Whether all are bound to perfect charity?
12. Whether charity, once possessed, can be lost?
13. Whether charity can be lost through one act of mortal sin?

ST. THOMAS AQUINAS

ON CHARITY

ARTICLE I

*Whether Charity Is Something Created in the Soul,
or Is it the Holy Spirit Itself?*[1]

It seems that charity is not something created in the soul.

1. For, as Augustine says,[2] just as the soul is the life of the body, so God is the life of the soul. But the soul is immediately the life of the body. Therefore God is immediately the life of the soul. Therefore, since a soul is said to be alive from the fact that it has charity, as is said (I *John* iii. 14), *He that loveth not, abideth in death,* man is not in charity through something which is a medium between God and man, but through God Himself. Charity, therefore, is not something created in the soul, but is God Himself.

2. But it was objected that the comparison is applied only in this respect, that the soul is the life of the body as a mover, and not insofar as it is the life of the body as a form. But on the contrary, in proportion as any agent is more powerful, to that extent it requires less of a disposition in the patient; e.g., the less dry the wood is, the greater must be the fire sufficient to burn it. But God is an agent of infinite power. Therefore, if He is the life of the soul, as moving it to love, it seems that no created disposition on the part of this soul is required.

3. Moreover, there is no medium among those things which are the same. But the soul loving God is the same as God, as is said (I *Cor.* vi. 17), *He who is joined to the Lord, is one in spirit.* Therefore no created charity comes as a medium between the soul loving and God being loved.

4. Moreover, the love by which we love our neighbor is charity. But the love by which we love our neighbor is God Himself, for Augustine says in Book VIII of the *De Trinit.*,[3] *He who loves his neighbor loves the same love.* But God is love. It follows, therefore, that he especially loves God. Therefore charity is not something created, but is God Himself.

5. But it was said that God, as a cause, is the love by which we love our neighbor. On the contrary, Augustine says in the same place,[4] and he

---

[1] See *Sum. Theol.* II-II, q. 23, a. 2; *In I Sent.* d. 17, q. 1, a. 1.
[2] See St. Augustine, *De Civitate Dei* XIX, 26; PL 41, 656.
[3] St. Augustine, *De Trinitate* VIII, 8; PL 42, 957.
[4] St. Augustine, *De Trinit.* VIII, 8; PL 42, 958.

clearly proved it with the testimony of the words of St. John, that that very celestial love by which we love each other is not only from God but also is God.[5] Therefore God is love not only causally, but essentially.

6. Moreover, Augustine says in Book V of the *De Trinitate*,[6] *For we are not going to say that God is called Love because love itself is a substance worthy of the name of God, but because it is a gift of God, as it is said of God, "Thou art my patience," in that He Himself gives it to us. For it is not said, O Lord You are my love; but it is said thus, "God is love," as it is said, "God is a Spirit."* Therefore it is that God is called charity not only causally, but also essentially.

7. Moreover, when the effect of God is known, He Himself is not known because of this, but He is known through the knowledge of the highest love. For Augustine says in Book VIII of the *De Trinit.*,[7] *For he knows the love with which he loves, more than the brother whom he loves. So now he can know God more than he knows his brother. Embrace the love of God, and by love embrace God.* Therefore God is called fraternal love not solely as a cause.

8. But it was objected that when fraternal love is recognized, God is recognized as in His own likeness. On the contrary, man is made in the image and likeness of God according to the very substance of his soul. But this likeness is obscured through sin. Therefore, in order that God be able to be recognized in the soul as in His own image, it is only necessary that sin be taken away, and not that some created thing be superadded to the soul.

9. Moreover, everything that is in the soul is either a potency, or a passion, or a habit, as is said in Book III of the *Ethic.*[8] But charity is not a potency of the soul, because if it were it would be natural. Nor is it a passion, because it is not in a sensitive potency in which are all passions. Nor is it a habit, because a habit is removed with difficulty;[9] charity, however, is easily lost through one act of mortal sin. Therefore charity is not something created in the soul.

10. Moreover, no created thing has infinite power. But charity has infinite power because it joins what is infinitely far apart, viz., the soul to God, and it merits an infinite good. Therefore charity is not something created in the soul.

11. Moreover, every creature is vanity, as is shown (*Eccle.* i. 2). Vanity, however, does not unite with truth. Therefore, since charity unites us to the First Truth, charity is not something created.

---

[5] St. Augustine, *De Trinit.* VIII, 8; PL 42, 958.
[6] St. Augustine, *De Trinit.* XV, 17; PL 42, 1080.
[7] St. Augustine, *De Trinit.* VIII, 8; PL 42, 957.
[8] Aristotle, *Nicomachean Ethics* II, 5, 1105b 20.
[9] See Aristotle, *Categories* VIII, 8b 30; *Nic. Eth.* VII, 10, 1152a 31.

12. Moreover, every created thing is a certain nature since it falls within one of the ten genera. Therefore, if charity is something created in the soul, it is a certain nature. Therefore, since we merit by charity, and if charity is a created thing, it follows that nature is the principle of meriting. This is the erroneous opinion of Pelagius.

13. Moreover, man is closer to God according to his existence in grace than he is according to his existence in nature. But God created man without a medium according to his existence in nature. So, neither in man's existence in grace does God use a medium, viz., a created charity.

14. Moreover, an agent which acts without a medium is more perfect than an agent which acts through a medium. But God is the most perfect agent. Therefore He acts without a medium. He does not, therefore, justify the soul through the medium of any created thing.

15. Moreover, a rational creature is more excellent than other creatures. But other creatures attain their own end without anything superadded. Therefore even more is a rational creature moved by God to its end without some created thing superadded to it.

16. But it was objected that a rational creature is not, through its own nature, proportionate to its end, and therefore it needs something superadded. On the contrary, the end of man is the infinite good. But no created thing is proportionate to an infinite good. Therefore that by which man is ordered to his end is not a good created in the soul.

17. Moreover, as God is the first light, He is also the highest good. But the light which is God is present to the soul, because of which it is said (*Ps.* xxxv. 10), *In thy light we shall see light.* Therefore the highest good, which is God, is also present to the soul. But the good is that by which we love something. Therefore that by which we love is God.

18. But it was objected that the good which is God is present to the soul not formally but efficiently. On the contrary, God is pure form. Therefore He is present formally in those things in which He is present.

19. Moreover, nothing is loved unless it is known, as Augustine says in Book X of the *De Trinitate*.[10] Therefore according to this, a thing is lovable according as it is knowable. But God is, through Himself, knowable as the first principle of knowledge. Therefore He is lovable through Himself and not through any created charity.

20. Moreover, a thing is lovable according as it is good. But God is infinite good. Therefore He is infinitely lovable. But no created love is infinite. Therefore, since some who have charity love God because He is lovable, the love by which we love God is not something created.

21. Moreover, God loves all things which exist, as is said (*Wis.* xi. 25). But He does not love irrational creatures through something superadded

[10] St. Augustine, *De Trinit.* X, 1 and 2; PL 42, 973 and 975.

to them; therefore neither does He love rational creatures in this way. Thus the charity and grace according to which man is loved by God is not something created and superadded to the soul.

22. Moreover, if charity is something created, it must be an accident. But charity is not an accident because no accident is more worthy than its subject. Charity, however, is more worthy than nature.[11] Therefore charity is not something created in the soul.

23. Moreover, as Bernard says,[12] we love God and our neighbor by the same law by which the Father and the Son love Themselves. But the Father and the Son love Themselves with an uncreated love. Therefore we love God with an uncreated love.

24. Moreover, that which can raise from death is of infinite power. But charity raises from death, for it is said (I *John* iii. 14), *We know that we have passed from death to life, because we love the brethren.* Therefore charity is of infinite power and is not something created.

On the contrary, everything which is received in a thing is received in it according to the mode of the receiver.[13] If, therefore, charity is received in us from God, it must be received finitely by us, according to our proper mode. However, every finite thing is created. Therefore charity is something created in us.

I answer. It must be said that there are some who have maintained that the charity in us by which we love God and our neighbor is nothing more than the Holy Spirit, as is clear from the Master in the First Book of the *Sent.*, dist. 17.[14]

In order that this opinion might be more clearly understood, it should be known that the Master placed this act of love by which we love God and our neighbor as a created thing in us, like the acts of the other virtues. But he set a difference between the act of charity and the acts of the other virtues. For, the Holy Spirit moves the soul to the acts of the other virtues by means of certain habitual means which are called virtues, but He moves the will immediately to the act of love through Himself without any habit, as is clear in Book I, dist. 17.[15] It was the excellence of charity which moved him to posit this theory, and the words of Augustine and others were used in objections. However, it was ridiculous to say that the very act of love which we express when we love God and our neighbor is the Holy Spirit Itself.

This opinion clearly cannot stand. For, just as natural actions and movements proceed from a certain intrinsic principle which is nature, so

[11] See *Sum Theol.* II-II, q. 23, a. 3, *ad.* 3m.
[12] See St. Bernard, *Sermones de Tempore* XXXIII; PL 183, 629.
[13] See *Sum. Theol.* I, q. 84, a. 1.
[14] *Petri Lombardi Libri IV Sententiarum* I, xvii, 1; I, 106.
[15] Peter Lombard, *Sent.* I, xvii, 1; I, 106.

also it is necessary that actions of the will proceed from an intrinsic principle. And, just as the natural inclination in natural things is called the natural appetite, so also in rational beings, the inclination which follows the apprehension of the intellect is the act of the will.[16]

It is, however, possible that a natural thing be moved not by an intrinsic principle but by some extrinsic agent, as for instance when a stone is thrown into the air. But it is certainly impossible that such a movement or action which does not proceed from an intrinsic principle be called natural, for this would imply a contradiction in itself. Whence, since for contradictories to exist at the same time does not lie within the divine power, it cannot even be effected by God that the upward motion of a stone, which does not proceed from an intrinsic principle, be natural to it. Now it is possible to give a stone that power by which it would naturally move upward as from an intrinsic principle, but that motion would not be natural to the stone unless another nature be given to it.

And likewise, it cannot be effected by God that any movement of man, either interior or exterior, which proceeds from an extrinsic principle be voluntary. Whence, all the acts of the will are reduced, as to a prime root, to that which man naturally wishes, which is the last end; and we wish the means for the sake of the end.

Therefore an act which exceeds the entire capabilities of human nature cannot be voluntary to man unless there be added to human nature something intrinsic, perfecting the will, so that such an action would proceed from an intrinsic principle.

If, therefore, the act of charity in man does not proceed from an interior habit superadded to a natural potency, but proceeds from the movement of the Holy Spirit, then one of these two alternatives follow: either that act of charity is not voluntary, which is impossible because to love something is to will it; or it does not exceed the capability of nature, and this view is heretical.

This difficulty being removed, it will follow, first, that the act of charity is an act of the will.[17] Secondly, if it is granted that the act of the will can be entirely from an extrinsic principle, as acts of the hands or feet, it will also follow that if the act of charity is only from the movement of an extrinsic principle, it cannot be meritorious. For, every agent which does not act according to its proper form but only because it is moved by another, is an agent only instrumentally, as an axe is an agent only inasmuch as it is moved by a woodsman.[18]

16 See *Sum. Theol.* I-II, q. 6, a. 1, *Resp.*
17 See *Sum. Theol.* II-II, q. 24, a. 1.
18 See *In IV Sent.* d. 1, q. 1, a. 4, qa. 1; *Sum. Theol.* I-II, q. 16, a. 1, *Resp.*; III, q. 19, a. 1, *ad* 2m; III, q. 62, a. 1, *ad.* 1m; *Quaestiones disputatae: De potentia Dei* q. 3, a. 4, *Resp.*; *De veritate* q. 26, a. 1.

[21]

Therefore if the soul does not effect an act of charity through some proper form, but only because it is moved by an extrinsic agent, i.e., by the Holy Spirit, then it will follow that it is considered only as an instrument for this act. There would not be, then, in man the power to act or not to act, and he would not be able to gain merit. For, only those things are meritorious which are in us according to a certain manner. Thus human merit is entirely taken away, since love is the basis of meriting.[19]

Thirdly it cannot hold, because it would follow that a man who is in charity would not be inclined to an act of charity, nor would he perform it with any pleasure. For, the acts of virtue are enjoyable to us because we are conformed to them according to a habit, and we are inclined toward them through the manner of a natural inclination. However, the act of charity is especially enjoyable and especially inclines one to remain in charity, and through it everything we do or suffer is rendered pleasing. The conclusion, therefore, is that there must be a certain habit of charity created in us, which is the formal principle of the act of love.

By this opinion it is not denied that the Holy Spirit, Who is Uncreated Charity, exists in man who has created charity, or that He moves man's soul to the act of love, as God moves all things to their own actions to which they are inclined by their own proper forms.[20] And thus it is that He disposes all things sweetly,[21] because to all things He gives forms and powers inclining them to that which He Himself moves them; so that they tend toward it not by force, but as if it were by their own free accord.

To the first, it must be said that God is the life of the soul in the manner of a mover, and not in the manner of a formal principle.

To the second, it must be said that although it pertains to the effectiveness of a mover that it does not require any disposition in the subject, however, that mover displays its effectiveness if it impresses a strong disposition in that which receives or is moved. For, a great fire causes not only substantial form to appear, but also a strong disposition. That agent which moves to action, and which also impresses a form through that which it moves, is stronger than that mover which so moves to action that it impresses no form. Therefore, because the Holy Spirit is the most powerful mover, He so moves to love that He also causes a habit of charity.

To the third, it must be said that when it is written (I *Cor.* vi. 17), *He who is joined to the Lord, is one in spirit*, this is not meant a unity of substance, but a unity of affection between the lover and the loved. By this union the habit of charity is regarded more as a principle of love than

[19] See *Sum. Theol.* I-II, q. 114, a. 4, *Resp.; De Virtutibus in Communi* a. 2. ad 18m.
[20] See *Sum. Theol.* II-II, q. 23. aa. 2-3.
[21] I have translated *suaviter* as sweetly. St. Thomas probably had this text in mind (*Wis.* viii. 1): *She reacheth therefore from end to end mightily, and ordereth all things sweetly.*

as a medium between the lover and the loved, for the act of love passes immediately to God as to the loved, but not immediately into the habit of charity.

To the fourth, it must be said that although the love by which we love our neighbor is God, it is however not denied that in addition to this uncreated love there is in us a created love by which we love formally, as has been said.

To the fifth, it must be said that God is said to be love or charity not only causally, as He is said to be hope or patience only causally, but also essentially. This, however, does not deny that besides that love which God is essentially, there is also in us a created love.[22]

The answer to the sixth objection is clear from the above.

To the seventh, it must be said that this text has the same difficulty whether a created habit of charity is posited in us or not. For, when Augustine said that he who loves his neighbor knows the love by which he loves more than he knows the neighbor whom he loves,[23] he seemed to understand the very act of love. Now no one holds that this act is something uncreated; therefore it cannot be concluded that the love thus known is God. Therefore when we perceive in ourselves an act of love, we feel a certain participation of God because God Himself is love, not because He is that very act of love which we perceive.

To the eighth, it must be said that a creature, insofar as it is more perfect, approaches more to a likeness to God. Whence, although any creature has a certain likeness to God in this, that it exists and is good, however a rational creature has, in addition, a further cause for similitude in this, that it is intellectual, and another in this, that it has been made. Thus in the act of charity God is more expressly perceived as in a closer likeness.

To the ninth, it must be answered that charity is a habit and is moved with difficulty.[24] For he who has charity is not easily inclined to sin, although charity is lost through sin.

To the tenth, it must be said that charity unites one to the infinite good not efficiently but formally, whence infinite power does not strive after charity, but rather the author of charity. However, infinite power would strive after charity if man were infinitely ordered to the infinite good through charity, which is clearly false. For, the manner follows the form of the thing.[25]

To the eleventh, it must be said that a creature is vanity because it

---

[22] See *Sum. Theol.* II-II, q. 23, a. 2.
[23] See St. Augustine, *De Trinit.* VIII, 8; PL 42, 957.
[24] See Aristotle, *Nic. Eth.* II, 3. 1105a 9.
[25] See *Sum. Theol.* I-II, q. 55, a. 2, *ad.* 1m; *Summa Contra Gentiles* III, 58.

is created out of nothing, not because it is a likeness of God; and it is for this reason that created charity unites to First Truth.

To the twelfth, it must be said that according to the Pelagian heresy, natural principles of man are sufficient for meriting eternal life. It is not, however, heretical to believe that we can merit by means of some created thing which exists as a certain nature in some category. For it is clear that we merit by our acts, and our acts, since they are certain created things, exist in some genus and are of a certain nature.

To the thirteenth, it must be said that God created natural being without an efficient medium, but not without a formal medium. For, to each thing He gave the form through which it exists. And likewise He gives existence in grace through some superadded form. But existence in nature and existence in grace are not entirely similar for, as St. Augustine says in *super Joan.*,[26] *He who created thee without thee will not justify thee without thee.* Therefore in justification, some operation of justifying is needed, and thus it is necessary that there be present an active formal principle, which is not present in creation.

To the fourteenth, it must be said that an agent acting mediately is less effective if he uses that medium because of its necessity. But God, in His acting, does not use a medium because He is in need of the help of any creature; He acts mediately in order that He might preserve order in things. But if we speak of a formal medium, it is clear that as the agent is more perfect, so much more will he induce a form. For an imperfect agent does not induce a form but only a disposition to the form, and the less perfect the agent is, the less is his power to induce that disposition.

To the fifteenth, it must be said that man and rational creatures are able to attain a higher end than do the other creatures. Whence, although they lack more things necessary to attain this end, nevertheless they are more perfect; just as a man who can attain perfect health through the use of several medicines is better disposed than one who is not able to be completely cured, even though he needs only a few prescriptions.

To the sixteenth, it must be said that the soul, through created charity, is raised above the possible limit of nature so that it might be ordered to a more perfect end than the capability of nature would supply. However, it is not so ordered to attain God perfectly, as He enjoys Himself perfectly. And this follows from the fact that no creature is proportionate to God.

To the seventeenth, it must be said that although the good which is God is through itself present to the soul, nevertheless there is need of a

---

[26] See St. Augustine, *In Joanis Evangelium* LXXII; PL 35, 1823; *Sermones* CLIX, 11; PL 38, 923.

formal medium—on the part of the soul, not however on the part of God—for the soul to be ordered perfectly to Him.

To the eighteenth, it must be replied that God is form subsisting essentially; He is not that which is joined as form to something else.[27]

To the nineteenth, it must be said that, granted that God is known through Himself by the soul—but this introduces another question—He is loved through Himself in the same way as He is known through Himself. When I say *through Himself*, this is understood on the part of the one loved, not of the one loving. For, God is loved by the soul not because of some other thing, but only because of Himself; and still the soul needs some formal principle in order to love God perfectly.

To the twentieth, it must be said that God cannot be loved by us to the extent that He is lovable, so that it does not follow that the love of charity by which we love God is infinite. This argument applies no less to an act than to a habit; but no one can say that the act of love by which we love God is something uncreated.

To the twenty-first, it must be said that we have need of a habit of charity insofar as we love God; this is not necessary for other creatures, although all creatures are loved by God.

To the twenty-second, it must be answered that no accident is more worthy than its subject as regards its manner of existing, because substance is being through itself, while accident is being existing in another.[28] But when the accident is an act and the form of the substance, there is nothing to prevent the accident from being more worthy than the substance. For in this way the accident is related to the substance as act to potency, as the perfect to the perfectible;[29] and it is thus that charity is more worthy than the soul.[30]

To the twenty-third, it must be said that although the law by which we love God and our neighbor is uncreated, that by which we formally love God and our neighbor is something created. For, the uncreated law is the first measure and rule of our love.

To the twenty-fourth, it must be said that charity revives the dead in a spiritual way, formally, but not as an effective agent. Therefore it is not necessary that it be of infinite power, since neither was the soul of Lazarus which, as a form, revived Lazarus inasmuch as he was revived through a union of his soul with his body.

---

[27] See *Sum. Theol.* II-II, q. 23, a. 2, *ad.* 3m.
[28] See Aristotle, *Posterior Analytics* I, 4, 73b 2; *Metaphysics* V (Δ), 7, 1017a 7.
[29] See Aristotle, *Metaph.* IX (Θ), 6, 1048a 25.
[30] See *Sum. Theol.* II-II, q. 23, a. 3, *ad.* 3m.

ARTICLE II

Whether Charity Is a Virtue?[1]

It seems that charity is not a virtue.

1. A virtue concerns what is difficult, according to the Philosopher in Book VI of the *Ethic.*[2] But charity does not pertain to the difficult; rather, as Augustine says in the *De Verbis Domini,*[3] *Love makes all hard and repulsive tasks easy and next to nothing.* Therefore charity is not a virtue.

2. But it was objected that what is done through virtue is difficult in the beginning but easy in the end. On the contrary, in the beginning there is not yet a virtue. If, therefore, it is difficult only in the beginning, virtue will not pertain to what is difficult.

3. Moreover, the difficulty in virtues arises from contraries, for it becomes difficult to preserve temperance because of the contrary concupiscences. But charity pertains to the highest good for which there is no contrary. Therefore that which pertains to charity is neither difficult in the end nor in the beginning.

4. Moreover, to esteem or to love is to wish a certain thing. But the Apostle says (*Rom.* vii. 18), *To will, is present with me.* Therefore to love is present to us. There is, therefore, required for this no other virtue of charity.

5. Moreover, in our mind there is only intellect and appetite. But the intellect is elevated to God by faith;[4] the affective power by hope.[5] It is, therefore, not necessary to posit a third virtue of charity to elevate the mind to God.

6. But it should be objected that hope elevates but does not join together, whence there is need for charity which will unite. On the contrary, hope, because it does not join, always concerns that which is not joined.[6] Hope is not necessary for those who are united to God through the enjoyment of beatitude. If charity unites, by the same reasoning it does not belong to those who are not yet united, i.e., to those living in this life. But virtue perfects us in this life, for it is a disposition of that which is perfect to that which is best.[7] Therefore charity is not a virtue.

7. Moreover, grace adequately joins us to God.[8] Therefore the virtue of charity is needed to unite us to God.

[1] See *Sum. Theol.* II-II, q. 23, a. 2; *In III Sent.* d. 27, q. 2, a. 2.
[2] Aristotle, *Nic. Eth.* II, 3, 1105a 9.
[3] St. Augustine, *Serm.* LXX, 3; PL 38, 444.
[4] See *Sum. Theol.* I-II, q. 62, a. 2; II-II, q. 4, a. 1.
[5] See *Sum. Theol.* II-II, q. 17, a. 2.
[6] See *Sum. Theol.* II-II, q. 17, a. 3.
[7] See Aristotle, *Physics* VII, 3, 246b 23.
[8] See *Sum. Theol.* I-II, q. 110, a. 3; *De veritate* q. 27, a. 2.

8. Moreover, charity is a certain friendship of man to God.[9] But friendship of man to man is not included by philosophers among the political virtues. Therefore the love of God ought not to be numbered among the theological virtues.

9. Moreover, no passion is a virtue.[10] Love is a passion, therefore it is not a virtue.

10. Moreover, virtue, according to the Philosopher, is a mean.[11] But charity is not a mean because there can be nothing beyond the love of God. Therefore charity is not a virtue.

11. Moreover, the affective power is corrupted more through sin than is the intellect, because sin is in the will, as Augustine says.[12] But our intellect is not able to see God in this state of life immediately as He is in Himself. Neither is our affective power able to love God in this state of life immediately as He is in Himself. But to love God as He is in Himself is attributed to charity. Therefore charity ought not to be numbered among the virtues which perfect us in this life.

12. Moreover, virtue is the ultimate limit of a power, as is said in Book I of the *de Caelo*.[13] But enjoyment is the ultimate limit which pertains to the affective power. Therefore enjoyment ought to be a greater virtue than love.

13. Moreover, every virtue has its proper measure; whence Augustine says that sin, which is the opposite of virtue, is a privation of mode, species and order.[14] But charity does not have a measure, because as Bernard says, the measure of charity is to love without measure.[15] Therefore charity is not a virtue.

14. Moreover, one virtue is not designated by another, because all the species of the same genus are divided through opposition. But charity is designated by the other virtues, for it is written (I *Cor*. xiii. 4), *Charity is patient, is kind*. Therefore charity is not a virtue.

15. Moreover, according to the Philosopher in Book VIII of the *Ethic.*,[16] friendship consists in a certain equality. But there is the greatest inequality between God and us, as between beings who are infinitely separated. Therefore there can be no friendship of God for us, or of us for God. So charity, which designates friendship of this kind, does not seem to be a virtue.

[9] See *Sum. Theol.* II-II, q. 23, a. 1.
[10] See *Sum. Theol.* I-II, q. 56, a. 4.
[11] See Aristotle, *Nic. Eth.* II, 6, 1106b 36.
[12] See St. Augustine, *De Duabus Animabus* X and XI; PL 32, 596.
[13] Aristotle, *On the Heavens* I, II, 281a 11.
[14] See St. Augustine, *De Natura Boni* III; PL 42, 553.
[15] See St. Bernard, *De Diligendo Deo* I; PL 182, 974.
[16] Aristotle, *Nic. Eth.* VIII, 8, 1159b 1.

16. Moreover, love of the highest good is natural to us. But virtue is not natural, because virtues are not in us by nature, as is clear from Book II of the *Ethic.*[17] Therefore love of the highest good, which is charity, is not a virtue.

17. Moreover, love is more excellent than fear. But fear, because of its own excellence, is not a virtue but a gift,[18] which is more excellent than a virtue. Therefore neither is charity a virtue but a gift.

On the contrary, the precepts of the law are about the acts of the virtues. Now the act of charity is commanded in the law, for it is written (*Matt.* xii. 37), that the first and greatest commandment is, *Love the Lord thy God.* Therefore charity is a virtue.

I answer. It must be said that charity is, without a doubt, a virtue. Now since a virtue is that which makes its possessor good and renders his works good,[19] it is clear that man is ordered to his proper good according to the proper virtue.

But the proper good of man must be considerd in various ways, according as man is understood under various aspects. The proper good of man as man is the good of reason, in that to be a man is to be rational.[20] But the good of man considered as an artist is the good of art; so also considered in his political character, his good is the common good of the state.

Since virtue operates for good, it is necessary for virtue of any kind that it operate well for the good, i.e., voluntarily, readily, with delight and firmly.[21] These are the conditions of virtuous operation which are not found in any operation unless the agent love the good for which he is working, because love is the principle of all the voluntary affective powers. For, that which is loved is desired when it is not possessed; there is pleasure when it is possessed; and those things which prevent one from having what has been loved cause sadness. Also, those things which are done out of love are done steadily, rapidly and with delight.[22] Therefore love of the good, for which virtue operates, is necessary for virtue.[23] But that virtue which belongs to man as man operates for a good that is connatural to man. Therefore the love of this good, which is the good of reason, is by nature in his will.

But if we accept the virtue of man according to some other consideration that is not natural to man, it will be necessary for virtue of this kind

---

17 Aristotle, *Nic. Eth.* II, 1, 1103a 24. See also St. Thomas, *Sum. Theol.* I-II, q. 63, a. 1; *De Virt. in Comm.* a. 13.
18 See *Sum. Theol.* II-II, q. 19, a. 9.
19 See Aristotle, *Nic. Eth.* II, 6, 1106a 15.
20 See *Sum. Theol.* I-II, q. 71, a. 6; II-II, q. 17, a. 1.
21 See *Sum. Theol.* I-II, q. 55, a. 1.
22 See St. Augustine, *De Diversis Quaestionibus* LXXXIII, q. 30; PL 42, 19.
23 See St. Augustine, *De Moribus Ecclesiae* I, 15; PL 32, 1322.

that love of that good to which such a virtue is ordered be something superadded to the nature of the will. For the artist does not operate well unless the love of the good which is intended through the operation of his art be added to him. Whence the Philosopher says in Book VIII of the *Polit.*,[24] for one to be considered politically good, he must love the good of the state.

But when man becomes a citizen of a state and is admitted to participating in the good of some state, certain virtues are suitable, necessary even, for doing those things which are a citizen's duty and for loving the good of the state. Therefore man, through grace, becomes as it were a citizen and a sharer in this blessed society which is called the heavenly Jerusalem (*Ephes.* ii. 19), *You are fellow-citizens with the saints, and the domestics of God.* And in this way, man is admitted to participating in celestial beatitude which consists in the vision and enjoyment of God.

Therefore certain gratuitous virtues, which are infused, are necessary for man when he is enrolled in the heavenly state; for the proper operation of these virtues there is required the love of the common good for the whole society, which is the divine good considered as the object of beatitude.[25]

But to love the good of any society involves a twofold consideration: first, the manner in which it is obtained; secondly, the manner in which it is preserved.

But to love the good of any society so that it might be had or possessed, does not constitute the political good. Thus does a tyrant love the good of the state in order to dominate it, which is to love himself more than the state; for he desires this good for himself, not for the state. But to love the good of the state so that it might be preserved and defended, this is indeed to love the state, and this constitutes the political good. So much is this so, that men would expose themselves to dangers of death or neglect their own private good, in order to preserve or increase the good of the state.[26]

Therefore, to love the good in which the blessed participate so that it might be had or possessed does not make man well-disposed toward beatitude, because the wicked also desire this good. But to love that good for its own sake in order that it might remain and be made wide-spread, and that nothing might act against that good, this does dispose man well toward that society of the blessed. This is charity, which loves God for His own sake, and loves fellow-men who are capable of attaining beatitude

---

[24] Aristotle, *Politics* VIII, 1, 1337a 27.
[25] See *Sum. Theol.* I-II, q. 51, a. 4; q. 62, a. 1; *In III Sent.* d. 33, q. 1, a. 2, qa. 3; *De Virt. in Comm.* a. 10.
[26] See Aristotle, *Nic. Eth.* I, 2, 1094b 8; *Politic.* I, 1, 1252a 1.

as it loves itself *(sicut seipsos);*[27] charity resists every hindrance both in itself and in others; charity can never exist with mortal sin,—that obstacle to beatitude.

Therefore it is clear that charity is not only a virtue, but even the most powerful of the virtues.[28]

To the first, it must be said that virtue does concern that which is difficult in itself, but it nevertheless becomes easy to one possessing virtue.

The answer to the second objection is clear from the above. But this remains: considered in itself, that with which virtue is concerned is difficult while it is in the process of coming to virtue. When it is virtuous it becomes easy, and this arises from the perfection of virtue.

To the third, it must be said that the difficulty is not only from contraries, but it is also from the excellence of the object. For, a thing is said to be difficult to understand for us because of the excellence of the intelligible, not because of some contrary.

To the fourth, it must be answered that the tendency which is present to us from nature is imperfect and weak as regards its freely obtaining things spiritual and gratuitous. For the Apostle also wrote in the same chapter (*Rom.* vii. 15), *I do not that good which I will.* Therefore there is need for the help of a gratuitous gift.

To the fifth, it must be said that hope lifts the affective power of man to the highest good so that it might be attained;[29] but in addition, it is necessary that this good be loved in order for it to be a good of man, as was said above in the body of the Article.

To the sixth, it must be said that, concerning the nature of charity or love, it is that which unites in affection.[30] For example, this union is considered in this respect: that a man consider his friend as another self, and wishes good for him as he does for himself.[31] But to unite in reality, this is not the nature of charity. Therefore there can be a love both of what is possessed and what is not possessed. It makes one desire what is not possessed, and be delighted with what is possessed.

To the seventh, it must be said that grace unites us with God in the manner of assimilation.[32] But it is necessary that we be made one with Him through the operation of the intellect and the will, which is done by charity.

---

[27] *Sicut seipsos* is corrupt. The idea clearly is that charity loves its fellow-men as it loves itself, using "charity" as equivalent to the "man who has charity."

[28] See *Sum. Theol.* II-II, q. 23, a. 6.

[29] See *Sum. Theol.* II-II, q. 17, a. 8.

[30] See St. Augustine, *De Mor. Eccl.* I, 11; PL 32, 1319.

[31] See Aristotle, *Rhetoric* II, 4, 1380b 35; 1381a 19; St. Thomas, *Sum. Theol.* II-II, q. 27, a. 2.

[32] See *Sum. Theol.* I-II, q. 110, a. 1; S.C.G. III, 150; *De Veritate,* q. 27, a. 1.

To the eighth, it must be answered that friendship is not posited as a virtue, but as something following virtue. For one who has virtue and loves the good of reason, it follows from the inclination of virtue that he loves what is like himself, i.e., virtuous men in whom the good of reason is strong. But the friendship which is for God, Who is blessed and the author of beatitude, ought to be included among the virtues which order men to beatitude. Therefore, since it is not consequent to the other virtues, but precedes them, as has just been shown, friendship must be in itself a virtue.

To the ninth, it must be said that love, considered in its sensitive part, is a passion; indeed, this is the love of the good through the senses. But such a love is not the love of charity, therefore the argument does not apply.

To the tenth, it must be replied that when the Philosopher said that virtue is a mean between two extremes,[33] he was referring to the moral virtues. This is not true of the theological virtues, among which is included charity, as has been shown in the preceding Question, Article 10.[34]

To the eleventh, it must be answered that something understood as good moves the will; and therefore, although the intellect knows God as the highest good through some medium, from this it moves the will so that He can be loved immediately although He is understood through some medium. For, that by which the knowledge of the intellect is determined, moves the will.

To the twelfth, it must be answered that enjoyment does not express the operation, but something consequent upon the operation. Now, since virtue is the principle of operation, enjoyment is not listed among the virtues, but among the fruits, as is shown (*Galat.* v. 22), *The fruit of the Spirit is, charity, joy, peace, patience.*

To the thirteenth, it must be said that the object of charity, viz., God, transcends every human capability. Whence, however the human will tries to love God, it is unable to reach Him so that it might love Him as much as He ought to be loved. Therefore it is said that charity has no measure, because there is no fixed terminus of divine love which, if love would exceed, would go against the nature of the virtue. But this can happen with the moral virtues which are means between extremes.[35] The measure of charity is this, that it has no such measure. It cannot be concluded from this that charity is not a virtue, but only that it does not stand as a mean like the moral virtues.

---

[33] See Aristotle, *Nic. Eth.* II, 6, 1106b 36.
[34] See *De Virt. in Comm.* a. 10.
[35] See Aristotle, *Nic. Eth.* II, 6, 1106b 36.

To the fourteenth, it must be said that charity is called patient and kind, as if named from the other virtues, inasmuch as it produces the acts of all the virtues.[36]

To the fifteenth, it must be said that charity is not a virtue of man considered as man, but of man as considered as becoming, through participation in grace, like to God and the Son of God, according to which it is written (I *John* iii. 1), *Behold what manner of charity the Father hath bestowed upon us, that we should be called, and should be the sons of God.*

To the sixteenth, it must be said that the love of the highest good, considered as the principle of natural being, is in us from nature. However, considered as the object of that beatitude which exceeds the total capacity of created nature, it is not in us from nature but is above nature.

To the seventeenth, it must be answered that the gifts perfect the virtues by raising them above the human way of acting. Thus, the gift of understanding perfects the virtue of faith;[37] and the gift of fear perfects the virtue of temperance from excesses that are beyond the human way of acting.[38] But in the love of God, there is no such imperfection which needs to be perfected by a gift. Therefore charity, which is more excellent than all the gifts, is not considered as the gift of virtue.[39]

[36] See *Sum. Theol.* Ii-II, q. 23, a. 8.
[37] See *Sum. Theol.* II-II, q. 8, a. 2.
[38] See *Sum. Theol.* II-II, q. 19, a. 9.
[39] See *Sum. Theol.* II-II, q. 23, a. 6.

ARTICLE III

Whether Charity Is the Form of the Virtues?[1]

It seems that charity is not the form of the virtues.

1. For, the form confers being and species on that of which it is the form.[2] But charity does not give being and species to any virtue. Therefore charity is not the form of the other virtues.

2. Moreover, there is no form of a form. All virtues are forms, for they are certain perfections. Therefore charity is not the form of the virtues.

3. Moreover, form is included in the definition of that of which it is the form.[3] But charity is not included in the definition of the virtues. Therefore charity is not the form of the virtues.

4. Moreover, those things which are separated by opposition are not so related that one is the form of the other. But charity is separated by opposition from the other virtues, as is clear (I *Cor.* xiii. 13), *And now there remain faith, hope, and charity, these three.* Therefore charity is not the form of the virtues.

5. But it must be objected that charity is not the intrinsic form of the virtues, but the exemplar. On the contrary, that which is in imitation of something derives its species from the exemplar.[4] Therefore, if charity is the exemplary form of all the virtues, all the virtues derive their species from it. Therefore all the virtues would be of one species, which is false.

6. Moreover, the form of the exemplar is that in imitation of which something is made;[5] therefore it is necessary only in order that a thing be made. If charity is the exemplary form of the virtues, charity itself will be necessary only for the generation of the virtues. Therefore, when the virtues are possessed, it will not be necessary to have charity, which is clearly false.

7. Moreover, the exemplar is necessary to make something,[6] but not to use what has already been made; just as the exemplar is necessary in transcribing a book, but not in using the book after it has been written. Therefore, if charity is the exemplary form of the virtues, it does not belong to us who use these virtues, but to God Who causes the virtues in us.

---

[1] See *Sum. Theol.* II-II, q. 23, a. 8; *In II Sent.* d. 26, q. 1, a. 4, *ad* 5m; *In III Sent.*, d. 23, q. 3, a. 1; d. 27, q. 2, a. 4, qa. 3; *De veritate* q. 14, a. 5; *De Malo* q. 7, a. 2.

[2] See Aristotle, *Phys.* II, 3, 194b 26; *Metaph.* V (Δ), 2, 1013a 27.

[3] See Aristotle, *Phys.* II, 3, 194b 26; *Metaph.* V (Δ), 2, 1013a 27.

[4] See Aristotle, *Phys.* II, 3, 194b 20; *Metaph.* V (Δ), 2, 1013a 30; VII (Z), 8, 1033b 30; *Sum. Theol.* I, q. 15, a. 3; *De veritate* q. 3, a. 1.

[5] See *De veritate* q. 3, a. 3, *ad* 3m.

[6] See *Sum. Theol.* I, q. 15, a. 3.

8. Moreover, the exemplar can exist without that which is made in imitation of it.[7] Therefore, if charity is the exemplary form of the virtues, it follows that it can exist without the other virtues, which is false.

9. Moreover, each virtue has its form from its end and object.[8] But that which is formed of itself has no need to be formed by another. Thus charity is not the form of the virtues.

10. Moreover, nature always produces that which is better. Therefore even more so does God. But it is better to be something formed than to be something without form. Since, therefore, God causes virtues in us, it seems that He produces them already formed; thus they do not need to be informed by charity.

11. Moreover, faith is a certain spiritual light.[9] But light is the form of everything which is seen in the light. Therefore, just as corporeal light is the form of colors, so also faith, and not charity, is the form of charity and of the other virtues.[10]

12. Moreover, the order of perfections is according to the order of perfectibles. But the virtues are perfections of the powers of the soul.[11] Therefore there is an order of virtues according to an order of powers. But among the powers of the soul, the intellect is higher than the will.[12] Therefore faith is higher than charity. And thus faith is more the form of charity than charity is of faith.

13. Moreover, just as the moral virtues are related to one another, so also are the theological virtues. But prudence, which is in the cognitive power, informs the other virtues, viz., justice, fortitude, temperance, and others of this kind which are in the appetitive power.[13] Therefore faith, which is in the cognitive power, informs charity, which is related to the appetitive power; and not the other way around.

14. Moreover, the form of a virtue is its measure.[14] But it is the role of the reason to determine the measure for the appetitive powers; and not the other way around. Therefore faith, which is in the reason, is more the form of charity, which is in the appetitive part, than is charity of faith.

15. Moreover, there is an interlinear note on this text (*Matt.* i. 2), *Abraham begot Isaac. And Isaac begot Jacob,* to this effect, that faith begot

---

[7] *Sum. Theol.* I, q. 15, a. 3.
[8] See *Sum. Theol.* I-II, q. 54, a. 2; q. 58, a. 3; q. 63, a. 4.
[9] See *Sum. Theol.* II-II, q. 4, a. 1; *De veritate* q. 14, a. 2.
[10] See *Sum. Theol.* I-II, q. 4, a. 3; q. 23, a. 8; *De veritate* q. 14, a. 5.
[11] See *Sum. Theol.* I-II, q. 61, a. 1.
[12] See *Sum Theol.* I, q. 82, a. 3; *De veritate* q. 22, a. 11; *S.C.G.* III, 26.
[13] See *Sum. Theol.* I-II, q. 61, a. 4; q. 66, a. 1.
[14] *Sum. Theol.* I-II, q. 61, a. 4; q. 66, a. 1.

hope, and hope begot charity. But everything produced receives its form from that which produces it.[15] Therefore charity receives its form from faith and hope; and not the other way around.

16. Moreover, in one and the same thing, potency precedes act in time.[16] Therefore, if charity is compared to the other virtues as act and form, it follows that in man the other virtues are prior in time to charity, which is false.

17. Moreover, the informing of moral matters has a relation to the end. But all the virtues are ordered, as to their final end, to the vision of God Who is complete reward, as Augustine says,[17] and Who takes the place of faith. Thus it seems that faith is the form of charity, rather than charity the form of faith.

18. Moreover, the final, efficient and formal causes do not coincide in number with one another, according to the Philosopher in Book II of the *Phys.*[18] But charity is the end and the mover of the virtues, therefore it is not the form of the virtues.

19. Moreover, the form is that from which comes the principle of being.[19] But the principle of spiritual being is grace (I *Cor.* xv. 10), *By the grace of God, I am what I am.* Therefore the grace of God, and not charity, is the form of the virtues.

On the contrary, St. Ambrose writes that charity is the form and the mother of the virtues.[20]

I answer. It must be said that charity is the form, the mover, and the root of the virtues.[21]

'To prove this, we should know that it is necessary to judge habits according to acts.[22] Wherefore, when that which pertains to one habit is as a form in regard to the act of another habit, then that one habit is related to the other as a form. But in all voluntary acts, that which has relation to the end is formal; this is so because any act receives its form and species according to the form of the agent, as the act of heating is according to the heat.[23]

However, the form of the will is its object, which is the good and the end, just as the intelligible is the form of the intellect. Therefore, that

---

[15] See Aristotle, *Phys.* II, 3, 194b 30; *Metaph.* V (Δ), 2, 1013a 30; VII (Z), 8, 1033b 30.
[16] See Aristotle, *Metaph.* IX (Θ), 7, 1049a 12.
[17] See St. Augustine, *De Mor. Eccl.* II, 3; PL 32, 1347.
[18] Aristotle, *Phys.* II, 7, 198a 24.
[19] See p. 33, n. 2.
[20] See Ambrosiaster, *In Epistolam B. Pauli ad Corinthios* 8, 2; PL 17, 239; *In Epistolam ad Romanos* 14. 1; PL 17, 175.
[21] See *Sum. Theol.* II-II, 23, 8; *De veritate* q. 14, a. 5.
[22] See Aristotle, *Nic. Eth.* II, 1, 1103a 31; St. Thomas, *Sum. Theol.* I-II, q. 51, a. 2.
[23] See p. 35, n. 15.

which has relation to the end must be formally in the act of the will. Thus in species, the same act is considered under the form of a virtue if it is ordered to one end, or under the form of a vice if it is ordered to another end. This is clear from the example of one who gives alms either for the sake of God or for the sake of vainglory.[24] For, the act of one vice, according as it is ordered to the end of another vice, receives the form of the second vice; e.g., he who would steal in order to commit adultery is a thief materially, but formally he is considered intemperate.[25]

It is clear that the act of all the other virtues is ordered to the proper end of charity, which is its object, viz., the highest good.[26] This is certainly clear regarding the moral virtues, for virtues of this kind are concerned with certain created goods which are ordered to the uncreated good as to their final end.[27] And the same is clearly evident regarding the theological virtues;[28] for uncreated being as true is indeed the object of faith; and insofar as it is desirable, it has the aspect of the good. Thus faith is directed toward that good insofar as it is desirable, since no one believes unless he wishes to believe. Even though the object of this species (i.e., the theological virtues) is uncreated being considered as good, nevertheless the object is still derived from the object of charity; for, the good is the object of hope insofar as it can be desired and obtained, since no one desires to obtain some good unless he loves it.

Therefore it is evident that in the acts of all the virtues there is the formal element which comes from charity; and it is called the form of all the virtues in that every act of all the virtues is ordered to the highest good that is loved, as has just been shown. And because the precepts of the law are concerned with the acts of the virtues, so it is that the Apostle writes (I *Tim.* i. 5), *The end of the commandment is charity.*

Thus it is apparent how charity can be the mover of all the virtues; it is the mover because it influences the acts of all the other virtues. For, every higher act or power is said to move a lower act or power, so that the act of the lower is ordered to the end of the higher.[29] For example, a house-builder commands a stone-mason so that the act of the stone-mason is ordered to the form of the house, which is the end of the builder. Since all the other virtues are ordered to the end of charity, charity commands the acts of all the virtues; and for this reason it is called their mover. And because the word "mother" signifies someone who receives and con-

[24] See *Sum. Theol.* I-II, q. 18, a. 4, *obj.* 3 and *ad* 3m.
[25] See Aristotle, *Nic. Eth.* V, 2, 1130a 24; St. Thomas, *Sum. Theol.* I-II, q. 18, a. 6.
[26] See *Sum. Theol.* II-II, q. 23, a. 7.
[27] See St. Augustine, *Epistolae* CLXVII; PL 33, 738; St. Thomas, *Sum. Theol.* I-II, q. 65, a. 3, *sed contra.*
[28] See *Sum. Theol.* I-II, q. 65, aa. 4-5; *De Virt. in Comm.* a. 10.
[29] See *Sum. Theol.* I, q. 77, a. 4.

ceives within herself, charity is called the mother of the virtues. For this same reason, charity is called the root of the virtues.[30]

To the first, it must be said that although charity does not give the proper species to any virtue, it gives, however, a common species to each virtue, on account of which we speak of virtue considered as the principle of meriting.

To the second, it must be said that there is no form of a form in the sense that one form is superior to the subject of another. But there is nothing to prevent several forms from existing in the same subject according to a certain order; so that one might be a proper form in respect to another, as color is the proper form in respect to what can be seen. It is in this way that charity can be the form of the other virtues.

To the third, it must be said that charity is included in the definition of a meritorious virtue, as is shown by the definition of Augustine,[31] who says that virtue is a good quality of the mind by which it lives rightly; for it does not live rightly unless it is through that which orders our life to God. This charity does.

To the fourth, it must be said that this argument follows from the form which enters into the constitution of a thing. Charity is not called the form of the virtues in this way but in another way, as has been shown above.[32]

To the fifth, it must be replied that charity, since it is the common form of the virtues, does indeed bring the virtues into one common species, a very special species, but not, however, into a proper species.

To the sixth, it must be said that charity can be called the exemplary form of the virtues; not an exemplar in whose likeness the virtues are generated, but an exemplar according to whose likeness the virtues operate in a certain way. Thus, whenever it is necessary to act according to virtue, charity is necessary.

To the seventh, it must be said that, although to create the virtues belongs only to God, however, to act according to virtue belongs also to a man possessing virtue. Therefore he needs charity.

To the eighth, it must be said that charity, considered as an act, not only is regarded as an exemplar, but also as a virtue which moves and causes. But the exemplar does not cause without producing that which is made in imitation of it, because it produces it in existence. And thus charity does not exist without the other virtues.

To the ninth, it must be said that each virtue has a special form from its proper end and its proper object, by which it becomes this virtue. But

[30] See *Sum. Theol.* II-II, q. 23, a. 8.
[31] See St. Augustine, *Contra Julianum* VI, 6; PL 44, 743.
[32] See the Reply to this Article.

it has from charity a certain common form, by which it can merit eternal life.

To the tenth, it must be answered that God makes the virtues in us that are formed with a special form and a general form. The special form is derived from the object and the end, but the general form is derived from charity.

To the eleventh, it must be said that light is the form of colors considered as visible in act through light; likewise, faith is the form of the virtues considered as knowable by us. For, we know by faith what is virtuous and what is not virtuous. But the virtues, insofar as they are operative, are informed by charity.

To the twelfth, it must be said that the intellect, considered in itself, is prior to the will, because the known good is the object of the will.[33] But in its operation and moving, the will is prior. For, the intellect does not understand or move unless the will gives its consent. Thus does the will move the intellect insofar as it is operative; for we use our intellect when we will.[34] Therefore, since to believe is an act of the intellect as moved by the will—for we believe something because we wish to—it follows that charity gives form to faith more so than faith to charity.

To the thirteenth, it must be said that the act of the will is considered according to the one who wills in relation to things as they are in themselves. But the act of the intellect is considered according as things known are in the one who understands. Whence, when things are below the one who understands, then the intellect is higher than the will,[35] because things exist in a higher manner in the intellect than in themselves, since everything which is in another is in it according to the manner of that in which it is. But when the things are above the one who understands, then the will rises higher than the intellect is able to attain.[36] Thus it is that in moral matters, which concern things below man, the cognitive virtue informs the appetitive virtues, just as prudence informs the other moral virtues.[37] But in the theological virtues which concern God, the virtue of the will, viz., charity, informs the virtue of the intellect, viz., faith.[38]

To the fourteenth, it must be said that rational power confers a way of desiring on those things which are below us, but not in those which are above us, as was said in Article I of this Question and in the preceding Question, Articles 10 and 11.[39]

[33] See *Sum. Theol.* I, q. 82, a. 4; *De veritate* q. 22, a. 11; *S.C.G.* III, 26.
[34] See *Sum. Theol.* I, q. 82, a. 4, *ad* 1m.
[35] *Sum. Theol.* I, q. 82, a. 4, *ad* 1m.
[36] *Sum. Theol.* I, q. 82, a. 4, *ad* 1m.
[37] See *Sum. Theol.* I-II, q. 61, a. 4; q. 66, a. 1.
[38] See *Sum. Theol.* II-II, q. 4, a. 3.
[39] *De Virt. in Comm.* aa. 10-11.

To the fifteenth, it must be answered that faith precedes hope, and hope precedes charity in the order of generation, as the imperfect precedes the perfect. But charity precedes both faith and hope in the order of perfection.[40] For this reason charity is said to be the form of them, as the perfect is the form of the imperfect.

To the sixteenth, it must be said that charity is not that form of the virtues which is a part of the essence of the virtues, so that it must follow the virtues or some matter of the virtues in time, as in the form of things generated. But charity is the form considered as informing; whence it must be, by its nature, prior to the other virtues.

To the seventeenth, it must be said that the vision of God, inasmuch as it is the end considered as a certain good, is the object of charity.

To the eighteenth, it must be said that the intrinsic form cannot be the end of a thing, although it is the end of the generation of a thing.[41] But charity is not the intrinsic form, as has been said; but from the fact that it brings the other virtues to their end, it forms the virtues, as is clear from what has been said.[42]

To the nineteenth, it must be said that the grace of God is called the form of the virtues according as it gives spiritual existence to the soul, so that it is able to receive the virtues. But charity is the form of the virtues according as it forms their operations, as was said in the body of the Article.

---

[40] See *Sum. Theol.* I-II, q. 66, a. 6; II-II, q. 23, a. 6; *De Virt. in Comm.* a. 10.
[41] See Aristotle, *Metaph.* VII (Z), 7, 1032a 15.
[42] See the Reply to this Article.

ARTICLE IV

Whether Charity Is One Virtue?[1]

It seems that charity is not one virtue.

1. Habits are distinguished by their acts; acts by their objects.[2] But charity has two objects; God and neighbor. Therefore charity is not one virtue but two.

2. It has been objected that one of these objects is more primary, viz., God, for charity loves fellow-man only on account of God. On the contrary, the Philosopher says in Book IX of the *Ethicor.*,[3] that friendly relations with another come from a man's relations to himself. But that which is a principle and cause is the most powerful in any genus. Therefore through charity man loves himself principally and God secondarily.

3. Moreover, it is written (I *John* iv. 20), *He that loveth not his brother, whom he seeth, how can he love God, whom he seeth not?* Therefore we ought to love our neighbor more than God. Since our neighbor is to be loved more than God, he is the more primary object of charity.

4. Moreover, nothing is loved unless it is known, as Augustine says in the *De Trin.*[4] But our neighbor is better known than God; therefore he is also loved more than God. Thus it seems that charity is not one virtue.

5. Moreover, every virtue has its own proper mode which it employs in regard to its acts; for a just man not only does just deeds, but also acts justly.[5] Charity uses two modes in its acts; for in charity one loves God with his whole heart, and he loves his neighbor as himself. Therefore charity is not one virtue.

6. Moreover, precepts of the law are ordered to the virtues, for the intention of the law-giver is to make men virtuous, as is seen in Book II of the *Ethicor.*[6] But two precepts are given for charity: *Love the Lord thy God, and love your neighbor.* Therefore charity is not one virtue.

7. Moreover, as we love God and our neighbor, so ought we to honor them. But we honor God and neighbor with different forms of honor; we honor God with adoration (*latria*), and our neighbor only with veneration (*dulia*).[7] Therefore there is one kind of charity by which we love God and another by which we love our fellow-men.

---

[1] See *Sum. Theol.* II-II, q. 23, a. 5; *In III Sent.* d. 27, q. 2, a. 4, qa. 1.
[2] See Aristotle, *Nic. Eth.* II, 1, 1103a 31; St. Thomas, *Sum. Theol.* I-II, q. 51, a. 2; q. 54, a. 2.
[3] Aristotle, *Nic. Eth.* IX, 4, 1166a 1.
[4] St. Augustine, *De Trinit.* X, 1 and 2; PL 42, 973 and 975.
[5] See Aristotle, *Nic. Eth.* V, 1, 1129a 7.
[6] Aristotle, *Nic. Eth.* II, 1, 1103b 3.
[7] See *Sum. Theol.* II-II, q. 25, a. 1, *obj.* 2 and *ad.* 2m.

8. Moreover, virtue is that by which we love rightly.[8] But to love God pertains to one life, to love neighbor pertains to another life; for to love God seems to belong to the contemplative life, while loving one's neighbor belongs to the active life. Therefore love of God and of our neighbor is not a single virtue.

9. Moreover, according to the Philosopher in Book I of the *Physic.*,[9] *one* is considered in three ways: as the continuous, as the indivisible, and as having the same essence. But charity does not have the unity of continuity because it is neither a body nor the form of a body. Nor has it the unity of indivisibility because then it would be neither finite nor infinite. Nor is it one in definition because synonymous things are one in this way, as *raiment* and *dress*. Therefore charity is not one.

10. Moreover, what is one by analogy is neither one in species nor in genus nor in number, as is said in Book V of the *Metaph.*;[10] even less are those things which are one only by analogy considered in the definition of the one. But charity is directed toward the eternal, viz., God and neighbor, who are not in the same relationship. Therefore in no way is charity considered one virtue.

11. Moreover, according to the Philosopher in Book VIII of the *Ethic.*,[11] perfect friendship cannot be had for many. But charity, by which God and neighbor are loved, is the most perfect friendship.[12] Therefore it is not directed to many. Thus God and neighbor are not loved with the same charity.

12. Moreover, a virtue, by the performance of which it is sufficient that we be not saddened, is different from a vitrue which is performed with pleasure; as fortitude is different from justice.[13] But in the act of charity, it is sufficient that we act without sadness in regard to some objects, as when we love our enemies; but it is necessary that we act with enjoyment in regard to others, as when we love God and our friends. Therefore charity is not one virtue, but different for each object.

On the contrary, (1) those things are one when they are so regarded that one thing is understood in another. But in loving our neighbor is understood the love of God, and vice versa, as Augustine says in Book VII of the *De Trinit.*[14] Therefore it is the same charity by which we love God and our neighbor.

---

[8] See St. Augustine, *Contra Julianum*, VI, 6; PL 44, 743; *De Libro Arbitrio* II, 19; PL 32, 1268.
[9] Aristotle, *Phys.* I, 2, 185b 7.
[10] Aristotle, *Metaph.* V (△), 6, 1016b 31.
[11] Aristotle, *Nic. Eth.* VIII, 3, 1156b 25.
[12] See *Sum. Theol.* II-II, q. 23, a. 1.
[13] See *Sum. Theol.* I-II, q. 61, a. 2; q. 61, a. 4.
[14] St. Augustine, *De Trinit.* VII, 7, 8; PL 42, 957.

(2) Moreover, in any genus, there is one first mover. But charity is the mover of all the virtues.[15] Therefore it is one.

I answer. It must be said that charity is one virtue.

To understand this, it must be said that any unity of power or of habit should be considered from the object, and this is because the potency is that which is said to have an order to the possible, which is the object. And thus the formal notion and the species of potency is taken from the object. It is the same for a habit, which is nothing more than a disposition of a perfected potency toward its object.[16]

In the object, however, something is considered as form, and something else as matter. The form in an object is that according to which the object is related to a potency or to a habit; but the matter is that in which the formal notion has its foundation. Thus, if we speak of the object of the power of sight, its formal object is color, or something of this kind, for according as a thing is colored, thus is it visible. Materially, however, it is the body in which the color exists.[17]

From this it is clear that a power or habit is related essentially to the formal notion of the object and only accidentally to the matter of the object. Whatever is accidental does not cause a change in the thing, but only that which is essential; therefore a material diversity in the object does not cause a diversity of power or habit because only a formal diversity causes this. There is one power of sight by which we see stones and men and the sky, because this diversity of objects is material and does not come from the formal notion of the visible. The sense of taste, however, differs from the sense of smell insofar as there is a difference between flavor and odor, which are sensibles in themselves.[18]

Now this consideration is necessary in regard to charity. It is evident that we can love something in a twofold way; in the first, by reason of its very self, and in the second by reason of another. We love someone for himself when we love him because of his proper good, viz., because he is essentially noble or because he is pleasing or useful to us. But we love someone for the sake of another when we love him because he is related to someone else whom we love. If we love someone on his own account, we love his entire family, his relatives, his friends, inasmuch as they are related to him; but in all of these, there is only one formal notion of love, viz., the good of the one whom we love for his own sake. And, in a certain way, we love him in all these others.

15 See *Sum. Theol.* II-II, q. 23, a. 8; *De veritate* q. 14, a. 5.
16 See Aristotle, *Nic. Eth.* II, 1, 1103a 31; St. Thomas, *Sum. Theol.* I, q. 77, a. 3; I-II, q. 51, a. 2; q. 54, a. 2.
17 See *Sum. Theol.* I, q. 77, a. 3.
18 *Sum. Theol.* I, q. 77, a. 3.

Therefore it must be said that charity loves God for His own sake; and because of Him, it loves all others according as they are ordered to God. Thus, in a way, charity loves God in all fellow-men, for our neighbor is loved by charity because God is in him or God might be in him. It is evident that it is the same habit of charity by which we love God and our neighbor.[19]

But if we love our neighbor for his own sake and not for the sake of God, this pertains to some other love, e.g., to a natural love, or a political love, or some other kind which the Philosopher discusses in Book VIII of the *Ethic*.[20]

To the first, it must be said that our neighbor is not loved except for the sake of God; whence formally considered, both are one object of love, although materially they are two.

To the second, it must be said that since love looks to the good, there is a diversity of love according as there is a diversity of the good.

There is, however, a certain good proper to each man considered as one person, and as far as loving this good is concerned, each one is the principal object of his own love. But there is a certain common good which pertains to this man or that man insofar as he is considered as part of a whole; thus there is a certain common good pertaining to a soldier considered as part of the army, or to a citizen as part of the state. As far as loving this common good is concerned, the principal object of love is that in which the good primarily exists; just as the good of the army is in the general, or the good of the state is in the king. Whence, it is the duty of a good soldier that he neglect even his own safety in order to save the good of his general. Thus also does a man naturally endanger his arm in order to save his head.[21]

And in this way charity regards the divine good as its principal object, which pertains to every one according as he is able to be a sharer in beatitude; thus we love out of charity only those objects which are able to participate in eternal happiness with us, as Augustine says in the *De Doctrina Christiana*.[22]

To the third, it must be said that St. John, denying the major premise, argues not that one's fellow-men ought to be loved more, but that they are more accessible to one's love, because men are more inclined to love what can be seen rather than the unseen.

To the fourth, it must be said that although what is known is loved, it does not follow that what is more known is also more loved. For, a thing

[19] See *Sum. Theol.* II-II, q. 25, a. 1.
[20] Aristotle, *Nic. Eth.* VIII, 3, 1156a 5.
[21] See Aristotle, *Nic. Eth.* I, 2, 1094b 8; *Politic.* I, 1, 1252a 1.
[22] St. Augustine, *De Doctrina Christiana* I, 27; PL 34, 29-30.

is not loved because it is known, but because it is good; thus that which is better is more lovable, even though it is not better known. For example, a man loves his servant or even his horse which he has had in constant use less than he loves some good man whom he knows only by reputation.

To the fifth, it must be said that charity regards the divine good as its formal object, as has been said in the previous Article and in the body of this Article. This good is related differently to God and to one's neighbor, therefore it is necessary that charity have a different mode as regards its primary and secondary objects. However, it has only one mode of operation in relation to its primary object.

To the sixth, it must be said that the precepts of the law concern the acts of the virtues and not the habits.[23] Therefore, from a diversity of precepts it does not follow that there is a diversity of habits, but only a diversity of acts. These acts pertain to one habit because of the formal notion.

To the seventh, it must be said that in honoring our neighbor we also honor his proper good; and thus one kind of honor is due to him, another kind to God.

To the eighth, it must be said that the love of neighbor as well as the love of God is included within the contemplative life, as Gregory writes in *Super Ezechiel*.[24] For prayer to God, which seems especially to pertain to the contemplative life, becomes prayer for fellow-man. So, too, the principle of the active life is, in a special way, the love of God in Himself. It does not follow, then, that if charity is the principle of different actions, it is not one.

To the ninth, it must be said that charity is not one by the unity of continuity, but it can be considered one by the unity of indivisibility inasmuch as it is one simple form. It is not called finite or infinite considered as a quantity with dimensions, but considered as the quantity of virtue.[25] Here we are not treating of charity in this manner, but only insofar as it is considered one in essence; not indeed a numerical unity as is *tunic* and *dress*, but a unity of species, as Socrates and Plato are one in their human nature.

To the tenth, it must be answered that this argument would hold if the object of charity be considered in its temporal aspect, not in its eternal aspect, as has been said.[26]

To the eleventh, it must be said that perfect friendship is not directed towards many, so that to each one it would be something proper to him-

---

[23] See *Sum. Theol.* I-II, q. 99, a. 2.
[24] St. Gregory the Great, *Super Ezechiel* II, Hom. 2; PL 76, 953.
[25] See *Sum. Theol.* II-II, q. 24, aa. 5-7.
[26] See the Reply to this Article.

self. But inasmuch as friendship towards one becomes more perfect as regards that one, the more perfect the love we have toward one, the better able are we to love others. Thus charity, because it is the most perfect friendship, extends itself to God and to all who are able to know God; it includes not only those whom we know, but also our enemies.[27]

To the twelfth, it must be said that virtue, which acts for its principal object with enjoyment, is able in the same way to act for some secondary object; not with pleasure, but without sadness. And in this way charity acts with pleasure towards its principal object, although with regard to a secondary object it endures difficulty in such a way that it is able to act without sadness.

[27] See *Sum. Theol.* II-II, q. 25, a. 8.

ARTICLE V

Whether Charity Is a Special Virtue Distinct From the Other Virtues?[1]

It seems that charity is not a special virtue.

1. That which is put in the definition of any virtue is not a special virtue, because a general virtue is included in the definition of each special virtue. But charity is included in the definition of each virtue, for Jerome says, *Let me briefly define all virtue as the charity by which we love God and our neighbor.*[2] Therefore charity is not a special virtue distinct from the others.

2. Moreover, charity by which we love our neighbor is not a virtue distinct from charity by which we love God; because charity loves fellow-man because of God.[3] But every virtue loves fellow-man because of God. Therefore no virtue is distinguished from charity.

3. Moreover, the distinctions of habits are marked by the acts of the virtues. But charity carries into effect the acts of all the other virtues, as is said (I *Cor.* xiii. 4), *Charity is patient, is kind.* Therefore charity is not a virtue distinct from the others.

4. Moreover, the good is the general object of all the virtues, for virtue is that which makes its possessor good and renders his works good.[4] But the good is the object of charity. Therefore charity has a general object, and thus it is a general virtue.

5. Moreover, a single perfection is of one perfectible. But charity is the perfection of many perfectibles, i.e., of all the virtues. Therefore charity is not one.

6. Moreover, the same habit cannot be in diverse subjects. But charity is in diverse subjects, for we are commanded to love God with our whole mind, with our whole soul, with our whole heart, and with our whole strength.[5] Therefore charity is not one virtue.

7. Moreover, charity is directed toward the removing of sins.[6] But charity is sufficient to take away all sins, because the least bit of charity can resist any temptation.[7] Therefore charity does that which belongs to all the virtues, and so does not seem to be a special virtue.

---

[1] See *Sum. Theol.* II-II, q. 23, a. 4; *In III Sent.* d. 27, q. 2, a. 4, qa. 2; *De malo* q. 7, a. 2; q. 9, a. 2.
[2] See St. Augustine, *Epist.* CLXVII; PL 33, 739.
[3] See *Sum. Theol.* II-II, q. 25, a. 1.
[4] See Aristotle, *Nic. Eth.* II, 6, 1106a 15.
[5] *Deut.* vi. 5; *Matt.* xxii. 37; *Mark* xii. 30; *Luke* x. 27. See *Sum. Theol.* II-II, q. 24, a. 1.
[6] See *Sum. Theol.* I-II, q. 55, a. 3.
[7] See *Sum. Theol.* II-II, q. 24, a. 8.

8. Moreover, some special sin is opposed to each special virtue. But all sins are contrary to charity, because charity is lost through each mortal sin.[8] Therefore charity is not a special virtue.

9. Moreover, no virtue is necessary except in acting uprightly. But charity alone sufficiently directs us in right acting, for Augustine says, *Have charity and do what you wish.*[9] Therefore there is no other virtue outside of charity; and charity is not a special virtue distinct from the others.

10. Moreover, the habits of the virtues are necessary in order that a man might act promptly and with enjoyment, for no one is just who does not rejoice in just works, as is said in Book I of the *Ethic.*[10] But charity is sufficient for the prompt and enjoyable operation of all works, for Augustine writes in the *De Verbis Domini,*[11] *Love makes all hard and repulsive tasks easy and next to nothing.* Therefore there is no need for any virtue outside of charity.

11. Moreover, those things which are distinct from each other have a distinct generation and a distinct corruption. But charity and the other virtues do not have distinct generations and corruptions because all the other virtues are communicated along with charity and they are lost when charity is lost.[12] Therefore charity is not a special virtue.

On the contrary, opposed to this is the fact that the Apostle (I *Cor.* xiii. 13) divides charity from the other virtues saying, *Now there remain faith, hope and charity, these three.*

I answer. It must be said that charity is a special virtue, distinct from the other virtues.

To understand this, it must be considered that whenever any act depends upon several principles that are constituted according to a certain order, it is necessary for the perfection of this act that each of the principles be perfect. For, if there be an imperfection in the beginning, or in the middle, or in the end, an imperfect act follows; just as if knowledge of art is lacking in the artist, or a right disposition be lacking in the instrument, an imperfect work will follow.[13]

And this can also be considered in the very powers of the soul. For, if right reason, which is the mover of the inferior powers, be correct, and the concupiscible attitude is disordered, one will indeed act according to reason, but the operation will be imperfect, for he will have hindrance from the ill-disposed concupiscence tending toward its contrary. This is

---

[8] See *Sum. Theol.* II-II, q. 24, a. 12.
[9] See St. Augustine, *In Epistolam Joannis ad Parthos* VII, 8; PL 35, 2033.
[10] Aristotle, *Nic. Eth.* I, 7, 1098a 7; II, 1, 1103b 1.
[11] St. Augustine, *Serm.* LXX, 3; PL 38, 444.
[12] See *Sum. Theol.* II-II, q .23, a. 7.
[13] See *Sum. Theol.* I-II, q. 57, a. 3.

clear in the example of the continent man.[14] Therefore in addition to prudence, which perfects reason, it is necessary in order that man be rightly constituted with regard to the objects of the concupiscible appetite, that he possess temperance in order that he might act readily and without hindrance.[15]

Just as among diverse powers, one of which moves the other, so one may consider diverse objects, one of which is ordered to the other as to an end. For, one and the same power, insofar as it is an end, not only moves another power, but even moves itself regarding the means to the end. Therefore, for right operation it is necessary that something not only be well-disposed toward the end, but also that it be well-disposed toward the means to the end. Otherwise, an impeded operation follows, as is clear in the case of one who is well-disposed toward attaining good health, but is ill-disposed toward undertaking the means which bring about health.[16]

Thus it is clear that, since man is disposed through charity to be well-ordered toward his final end, it is necessary to have other virtues by which he will be well-disposed toward the means which pertain to the end. Charity, therefore, is different from the virtues which are ordered to the means to the end; even though that virtue which is ordered to the end is more primary and architectonic with respect to the other virtues, which are ordered to the means to the end.[17] In this way, medical knowledge is related to the art of applying unguents, or the military art is related to horsemanship.

It becomes clear, therefore, that it is necessary for charity to be a special virtue, distinct from the other virtues, but yet the most important virtue and the mover of the other virtues.

To the first, it must be said that this is a causal definition inasmuch as charity is the cause of the other virtues.

To the second, it must be answered that charity in loving fellow-man has God as the formal notion of the object, and not only as the final end, as it clear from the preceding Article. The other virtues have God, not as the formal notion of the object, but as their final end.

Thus, when it is said that charity loves neighbor on account of God, the *on account of* denotes not only the material cause, but in a way the formal cause. But when it is said of the other virtues that they operate on account of God, the *on account of* denotes only the final cause.

To the third, it must be said that charity does not produce the acts of the other virtues by eliciting them, but only by commanding them. For,

[14] See Aristotle, *Nic. Eth.* VII, 3, 1147b 1.
[15] See *Sum Theol.* I-II, q. 61, aa. 2-3.
[16] See Aristotle, *Nic. Eth.* III, 2, 1111b 26; *Sum. Theol.* I, q. 83; a. 4; I-II, q. 8, aa. 2-3; q. 12, a. 4; q. 56, a. 6; *De veritate* q. 22, aa. 14-15.
[17] See *Sum. Theol.* I-II, q. 62, a. 1; q. 65, a. 2.

the virtue draws out only those acts which are according to the notion of proper form, as justice acts rightly or temperance acts temperately. But virtue is said to command all the acts which it summons up to its end.

To the fourth, it must be said that the good in general is not the object of charity, but the highest good. Therefore it does not follow that charity is a general virtue, but that it is the highest virtue.

To the fifth, it must be said that charity is not the intrinsic perfection of the other virtues, but the extrinsic perfection, as was said in Article III of this Question. Therefore the objection does not follow.

To the sixth, it must be said that charity exists as in a subject in only one power, viz., the will which, through its command, moves the other powers.[18] According to this, we are commanded to love God with our whole mind and our whole soul in order that all the powers of our soul might be summoned in submission to divine love.

To the seventh, it must be said that, just as charity commands the acts of the other virtues, so through this manner of commanding does it exclude the sins which are contrary to these virtues; and in this way charity resists temptations.[19] However, it is necessary that there be other virtues which directly and in an elicited way drive out sins.[20]

To the eighth, it must be said that, just as the acts of the other virtues are ordered to the end which is the object of charity, so also do sins, which are contrary to those virtues, oppose the end which is the object of charity.[21] From this it happens that the contraries of the other virtues, viz., sins, drive out charity.

To the ninth, it must be said that, although charity adequately directs us through its manner of commanding in all things which pertain to a righteous life, nevertheless other virtues are required which, by eliciting their acts, carry out the command of charity so that man will act readily and without impediment.

To the tenth, it must be said that it sometimes happens that a thing which in itself is difficult and causes sadness may exist for the sake of an end; as one freely takes a bitter medicine for the sake of health, although he is much afflicted by its consumption. Charity, therefore, makes all things pleasing in respect to the end, but the other virtues are needed which make those things which are good in themselves more enjoyable, in order that we may more easily do them.

To the eleventh, it must be said that charity is generated at the same time as the other virtues, not because it is not distinct from the others, but because the works of God are perfect. Whence, when charity is com-

[18] See *Sum. Theol.* I-II, q. 56, a. 6; II-II, q. 24, a. 1; *De Virt. in Comm.* a. 5.
[19] See *Sum. Theol.* II-II, q. 24, a. 8.
[20] See *Sum. Theol.* I-II, q. 74, a. 2.
[21] See *Sum. Theol.* I-II, q. 71, a. 4; II-II, q. 23, a. 8; II-II, q. 24, a. 10.

municated, all the virtues which are necessary for salvation are communicated at the same time.[22] However, charity is corrupted at the same time as the virtues because whatever is opposed to the other virtues is opposed to charity, as has been said.[23]

[22] See *Sum. Theol.* I-II, q. 71, a. 4; II-II, q. 23, a. 8.
[23] See the Reply to the eighth objection of this Article.

ARTICLE VI

Whether There Can Be Charity With Mortal Sin?[1]

It seems that charity can exist with mortal sin.

1. Origen says in *I Periarchon.,*[2] *I do not think that anyone who has continually stayed in the highest and perfect state would suddenly fall from that height, but he must needs fall away little by little.* But one commits mortal sin suddenly, through his consent alone. Therefore he who is in a perfect state through charity cannot fall away from charity through one act of mortal sin. Thus charity can exist along with mortal sin.[3]

2. Moreover, Bernard says that the charity in Peter when he denied Christ was not wiped out, but only rendered inactive.[4] But Peter, by denying Christ, sinned mortally. Therefore charity can remain with mortal sin.

3. Moreover, charity is stronger than the habit of a moral virtue. But the habit of virtue is not taken away through one act of vice, since it is not generated through one act; for virtue is generated and corrupted by doing the same things in a contrary manner, as is said in Book II of the *Ethic.*[5] Therefore much less is the habit of charity taken away through a single mortal sin.

4. Moreover, to each thing there is one thing in opposition. But charity is a special virtue, as has been shown.[6] Therefore there is opposed to it one special vice. Thus charity is not taken away by other mortal sins, and so it seems that it is possible for mortal sin to exist along with charity.

5. Moreover, things in opposition cannot be in the same subject, for one drives out the other. But some sins are not in the same subject with charity, for charity is in the higher reason which is turned to God; but mortal sin can exist in the lower reason, as Augustine says in the *De Trinit.*[7] Therefore not every mortal sin drives out charity.

6. Moreover, that which is the strongest is not able to be driven out by what is the weakest. But charity is the strongest, for it is said (*Cantic.* viii. 6), *Love is strong as death.* But sin is the weakest because evil is infirm and powerless, as Dionysius says.[8] Therefore mortal sin does not drive out charity, and so it can exist along with it.

---

[1] See *Sum. Theol.* I-II, q. 52 a. 1; q. 66, a. 1; II-II, q. 24, a. 4; q. 24, a. 5; q. 24, a. 12; *In I Sent.* d. 17, q. 2, a. 1; *De malo,* q. 7, a. 2; *Quaestiones Quodlibetales* IX, a. 6.

[2] Origen, *Peri Archon* I, 3; PG 11, 155.

[3] See *Sum. Theol.* II-II, q. 24, a. 12.

[4] See William of St. Thierry, *De Natura et Dignitate Amoris* VI; PL 184, 390.

[5] Aristotle, *Nic. Eth.* II, 1, 1103b 8; II, 3, 1105a 14.

[6] See Article V of this Question.

[7] St. Augustine, *De Trinit.* XII, 12; PL 42, 1008.

[8] See Dionysius, *De Divinis Nominibus* IV, 32; PG 3, 732.

7. Moreover, habits are known through their acts.[9] But the act of charity is able to exist with mortal sin, for a man sinning loves God and his neighbor. Therefore charity can exist with mortal sin.

8. Moreover, charity especially causes one to take delight in the contemplation of God. But there is no contrary to that delight which comes from speculative knowledge, as the Philosopher says in Book I of the *Topic*.[10] Therefore there is no contrary to charity, and so it is not able to be driven out by mortal sin.

9. Moreover, a universal mover can be hindered in regard to one object that is potentially movable, and not in regard to another. But charity is the universal mover of all the virtues, as was said above in Article III. Therefore it is not necessary that its operation towards one virtue be hindered insofar as it moves the others. Thus charity is able to exist with the sin which is opposed to temperance, according as it is the mover of the other virtues.

10. Moreover, just as charity has God as its object, so too do faith and hope. But faith and hope are able to exist without form; so too, therefore, is charity.[11] Thus it is able to exist with mortal sin.

11. Moreover, everything which does not have the perfection it was meant to have by nature is without form. But charity does not have here in this life the perfection that it is destined to have in heaven.[12] Therefore it is without form, and thus it seems that it can exist with mortal sin.

12. Moreover, habits are known through acts.[13] But some acts of those who have charity can be imperfect; for oftentimes those who have charity are moved by another movement to impatience, or to vainglory.[14] Therefore it may happen that the habit of charity is imperfect and without form, and thus it seems that mortal sin can exist with charity.

13. Moreover, just as sin is opposed to virtue, so is ignorance opposed to science. But not every ignorance takes away complete science.[15] Therefore not every mortal sin takes away all virtue. Whence, since charity is the root of the virtues, it does not seem that every mortal sin takes away charity.

14. Moreover, charity is the love of God. But a person who keeps his love towards a thing can act against it through incontinence; just as one loving himself acts against his good through incontinence; and another loving his community acts against it through incontinence, as the Philo-

[9] See Aristotle, *Nic. Eth.* II, 1, 1103a 31; St. Thomas *Sum. Theol.* I-II, q. 51, a. 2.
[10] Aristotle, *Topics* I, 15, 106a 36.
[11] See *Sum. Theol.* I-II, q. 62, a. 3; II-II, q. 23, a. 6; q. 25, a. 1; *De veritate* q. 14, a. 5, *sed contra; De Virt. in Comm.* aa. 10-11.
[12] See *Sum. Theol.* II-II, q. 24, a. 8; q. 27, a. 4.
[13] See Aristotle, *Nic. Eth.* II, 1, 1103a 31; St. Thomas, *Sum. Theol.* I-II, q. 51, a. 2.
[14] See *Sum. Theol.* II-II, q. 23, a. 7; q. 24, a. 10; q. 24, a. 12.
[15] See *Sum. Theol.* I-II, q. 76, aa. 1-3.

sopher says in Book V of the *Politic.*[16] Therefore one can act against God by sinning and still remain in charity.

15. Moreover, one can be well-disposed toward the universal, and yet fail in the particular. For example, the incontinent man has right reason toward the universal, viz., that it is wrong to commit fornication; but yet in regard to the particular, he chooses here and now to commit fornication as a good, as is explained by the Philosopher in Book VI of the *Ethic.*[17] But charity causes man to keep himself well-disposed toward the universal end. Therefore, remaining in charity, one can sin in regard to some particular act, and thus charity can exist with mortal sin.

16. Moreover, contraries are in the same genus. But sin is in the genus of act because sin is something said, done, or desired contrary to the law of God.[18] But charity is in the genus of habit. Therefore sin is not contrary to charity, and so does not drive out charity. It is, therefore, able to exist with charity.

On the contrary, (1) it is said (*Wis.* i. 5), *For the Holy Spirit of discipline will flee from the deceitful, and will withdraw himself from thoughts that are without understanding, he shall not abide when iniquity cometh in.* But the Holy Spirit is in man as long as he has charity, because the Spirit of God dwells in us through charity. Therefore charity is driven out when sin enters, and thus it is not able to exist along with mortal sin.[19]

(2) Moreover, whoever has charity is worthy of eternal life, according to the Apostle (II *Tim.* iv. 8), *There is laid up for me a crown of justice, which the Lord the just judge will render to me in that day: and not only to me, but to them also that love his coming.* However, whoever sins mortally is worthy of eternal punishment, according to what is written (*Rom.* vi. 23), *The wages of sin is death.* But no one can at the same time be worthy of eternal life and of eternal punishment. Therefore charity cannot be retained with mortal sin.

I answer. It must be said that charity can, in no way, exist along with mortal sin.

To prove this, it must be considered, first, that every mortal sin is directly opposed to charity. Whoever chooses something in preference to something else, loves better that which he first chooses. Whence, because man loves his own life and his own continuance more than pleasure, however great that pleasure may be, he is drawn away from pleasure if he thinks that it is infallibly destructive of his own life. This is ex-

---

[16] Aristotle, *Politic.* V, 5, 1304b 20.
[17] Aristotle, *Nic. Eth.* VII, 1, 1145b 12.
[18] See *Sum. Theol.* I-II, q. 71, a. 6.
[19] See *Sum. Theol.* I-II, q. 88, a. 3.

plained by Augustine when he writes in the LXXXIII *Quaestionum*[20] that there is no one who fears pain more than he who seeks pleasure. Sometimes we even see that the most savage of beasts will avoid the greatest pleasures because of the fear of pain.

However, one sins mortally in this, that he prefers something other than to live according to God and to cling to God. Thus it is clear that whoever sins mortally, by this fact he loves some other good more than he loves God; for if he would love God, he would choose to live according to God more than to obtain some temporal good. However, it is of the very essence of charity that God be loved above all things, as is clear from what is said above.[21] Therefore every mortal sin is contrary to charity.[22]

Charity is founded in man by God. But those things which are caused by divine infusion are in need of divine action not only in the beginning so that they might begin to exist, but also in their entire duration so that they might be preserved in existence. For example, the illumination of the air needs the presence of the sun not only when the air is first lighted, but as long as it remains lighted. And for this reason, if any intervening obstacle prevents the direct rays of the sun, the light in the air fails. Likewise, when mortal sin enters, which obstructs the soul's direct sight of God—and through this something else is preferred to God—the flow of charity is stopped, and charity is then lacking in man, as is said (*Isaias*. lix. 2), *Your iniquities have divided between you and your God.*

But when the mind of man again returns to God by regarding Him rightly and by loving Him above all things—which, however, cannot be done without divine grace—man immediately returns again to charity.[23]

To the first, it must be said that the words of Origen[24] should not be understood to mean that a man sinning mortally, howsoever perfect he was, does not suddenly lose charity. The words are to be interpreted to mean that it does not easily happen that a perfect man would suddenly commit a mortal sin at once, but through negligence; and many venial sins would be disposed finally to fall into mortal sin.

To the second, it must be answered that the text of Bernard[25] does not seem to hold unless it be understood that charity was not extinct in Peter, only because it was soon resurrected; for those things which are

---

[20] St. Augustine, *Lib.* 83 *Quaest.* q. 36; PL 40, 25.
[21] See the *sed contra* of this Article.
[22] See *Sum. Theol.* II-II, q. 24, a. 12.
[23] See *Sum. Theol.* I-II, q. 62, a. 2; *De Virt in Comm.* aa. 10-11.
[24] See Origen, *Peri Archon* I, 3; PG 11, 155.
[25] See William of St. Thierry, *De Nat. et Dign. Amoris* VI; PL 184, 390.

not very far apart seem as if they are not separated at all, as is said in Book II of the *Physic*.[26]

To the third, it must be said that a moral virtue which is acquired by acts consists in an inclination of power to act; and that inclination is not entirely taken away by one act.[27] But by one act, the influence that God exerts in the operation of charity is taken away; therefore one act of sin takes away charity.

To the fourth, it must be said that, in general, the opposite of charity is hate;[28] but indirectly all sins are opposed to charity insofar as they pertain to the contempt of God Who ought to be loved above all things.

To the fifth, it must be said that the higher reason, in which charity exists, moves the lower reason. Therefore sin, inasmuch as it is opposed to the movement of charity in the lower part of the soul, drives out charity. Or, it can be answered that mortal sin does not exist without consent, which is attributed to the higher faculty of reason in which charity exists.[29]

To the sixth, it must be said that sin does not drive out charity by its own power, but only in virtue of the fact that man voluntarily subjects himself to sin.

To the seventh, it must be said that a man who sins mortally does not love God above all things, as He ought to be loved in charity; but there is something else that he prefers to the love of God, and on account of this thing, he despises the law of God.

To the eighth, it must be said that delight, which comes from speculative knowledge, does not have a contrary in the same genus so that the consideration of some other thing would be contrary to it.[30] This is because the species of contraries are not contrary in the understanding; whence, the delight which comes from a consideration of *white* is not contrary to the delight which comes from a consideration of *black*. Since the act of the will consists in the movement of the soul toward the thing willed, and just as things in themselves are contraries, so the movements of the will towards these contraries are contraries. For, the desire of sweetness is contrary to the desire of the bitter. According to this, the love of God is contrary to the love of sin which excludes one from God. However, speculative knowledge, insofar as there is no contrary, is not a proper act of charity which is elicited by it, but charity is only commanded by it as its effect.

---

[26] Aristotle, *Phys.* II, 3, 195a 30.
[27] See *Sum. Theol.* I-II, q. 65, a. 1.
[28] See *Sum. Theol.* II-II, q. 34, a. 2.
[29] See *Sum. Theol.* I-II, q. 74, a. 7.
[30] See Aristotle, *Topics* I, 15, 106a 36.

To the ninth, it must be said that charity which is the universal mover of the virtues, when it is impeded through mortal sin in regard to those things which pertain to one virtue, is impeded in regard to its own universal object; and because of this it is universally impeded in regard to all.[31] However, this is not true when the object that is potentially movable is so hindered in regard to its particular effect, so that it is not hindered in regard to those things which pertain to universal virtue.

To the tenth, it must be said that although hope and faith have God as their object, they are not the form of the other virtues; as is true of charity and as was proved above in Article III. Therefore, although charity is not without form, hope and faith can exist without form.

To the eleventh, it must be said that a defect of any perfection does not render virtue without form, but only that defect which removes the order to the final end. Indeed, there is an order in the charity of this life, although the charity of this life does not have the perfection of the charity of heaven which is in accord with its proper and perfect enjoyment of God.[32]

To the twelfth, it must be said that imperfect acts can be performed by one possessing charity, but they do not follow from charity.[33] For, not every act of the agent is the act of each form in the agent, and this is especially true in a rational nature which possesses freedom to exercise those habits in it.

To the thirteenth, it must be said that although not every ignorance of proper principles excludes science, however the ignorance of common principles does take away science, and when these principles are unknown, it follows that there is an ignorance of art, as is said in Book I of the *Elench*.[34] However, the final end is regarded as the most common principle to all. Therefore, a de-ordination from the final end through mortal sin completely removes charity. But every de-ordination of particular principles does not remove charity, as is clear with venial sins.

To the fourteenth, it must be said that whoever acts incontinently against a good which he loves, thinks that the good is not completely lost through that incontinent act which he is doing. For, if anyone who loves a certain state, or the health of his own body, would think that he would lose either of these through what he is doing, he would either abstain totally from those acts, or he would love that which he did more than his health or the good of the state.[35] Whence, although one knows that

---

[31] See *Sum. Theol.* II-II, q. 24, a. 10.
[32] See *Sum. Theol.* II-II, q. 24, a. 8.
[33] See *Sum. Theol.* II-II, q. 24, a. 9.
[34] Aristotle, *On Sophistical Refutations* I, 165a 20.
[35] See Aristotle, *Politic.* V, 5, 1304b 20.

he loses God through mortal sin—which is to know that he has sinned mortally—and nevertheless is doing that incontinent act, he clearly loves what he is doing more than he loves God.

To the fifteenth, it must be said that charity requires not only that there be a disposition to the universal, that God be loved above all things, but also that the act of choice and of the will be so disposed toward any particular that is chosen. And this particular choice is excluded through the choice of the contrary, viz., sin, which excludes one from God.

To the sixteenth, it must be answered that although acts are directly contrary to acts, and habits to habits, acts are also indirectly contrary to habits according as they conform to contrary habits. For, similar acts are generated from similar habits, and similar acts cause similar habits; although not all habits are caused by acts.[36]

---

[36] See *Sum. Theol.* I-II, q. 51, aa. 1-3.

ARTICLE VII

Whether the Object to Be Loved Out of Charity Is a Rational Nature?[1]

It seems that the object to be loved out of charity is not a rational nature.

1. That because of which a thing is so is itself more so.[2] But man is loved in charity because of his virtue and blessedness. Therefore virtue and blessedness, which are not rational creatures, are more to be loved in charity; and thus a rational creature is not the proper object of charity.

2. Moreover, through charity we are made especially like to God in our loving. But God loves all things that are, as is said (*Wis.* xi. 25), by loving Himself, Who is Love, in charity. Therefore not only a rational nature, but all things are to be loved in charity.

3. Moreover, Origen says in *Super Cantica*,[3] that it is one thing to love God and every other good. But God is loved in charity. Therefore, since all creatures are good, not only the rational nature but all creatures are to be loved in charity.

4. Moreover, only the love of charity is meritorious.[4] But we can merit in the love of any thing. Therefore we can love any thing out of charity.

5. Moreover, God is loved out of charity. Therefore that ought to be more loved out of charity which is especially loved by Him. But among all created things, the good of the universe, in which all things are included, is especially loved by God. Therefore all things are to be loved in charity.

6. Moreover, to love more pertains to charity than does to believe. But charity believes all things, as is said (I *Cor.* xiii. 7). Therefore much more should charity love all things.

7. Moreover, rational nature is found most perfectly in God. If, therefore, a rational nature is the object of charity, it would be necessary that we love God in charity. But this seems impossible, since the love of charity is a perfect love. We cannot love God perfectly in this life because we do not know Him perfectly in this life; and we do not know what God is but only what He is not.[5] But love presupposes knowledge, since nothing is loved unless it is known.[6] Therefore a rational or intellectual nature is not the proper object of charity.

---

[1] See *Sum. Theol.* II-II, q. 25, a. 3; *In III Sent.* d. 28, q. 1, a. 2.
[2] See Aristotle, *Post. Anal.* I, 2, 72a 29.
[3] Origen, *In Canticum Canticorum* Hom. II; PG 13, 64.
[4] See *Sum. Theol.* I-II, q. 114, a. 4; *De Virt. in Comm.* a. 2, ad 18m.
[5] See *Sum. Theol.* II-II, q. 24, a. 8.
[6] See St. Augustine, *De Trinit.* X, 1 and 2; PL 42, 973 and 975.

8. Moreover, God is farther from man than is any creature other than man. If, then, we do not love other creatures in charity, much less are we able to love God out of charity.

9. Moreover, intellectual nature is also found in angels. But it seems that angels do not have to be loved out of charity. Therefore intellectual nature is not the proper object of charity. The proof of the minor is given: friendship consists in a sharing of life, for, according to the Philosopher in the *Ethicor.*,[7] to live together is proper to friends. But there does not seem to be any sharing of life between the angels and us, because we do not share with the angels in the life of nature, for they are more excellent in nature than man. Nor, again, do we share with them in the life of glory, for the gifts of grace and of glory are given by God according to the active capacity of the one receiving, as is said (*Matt.* xxv. 15), *To every one He gave according to his proper ability.* But the capacity for action of the angel is much greater than that of man. Therefore the angels do not share with men in any life.

10. Moreover, rational nature is also found in the same man loving out of charity. But it seems that man ought not to love himself out of charity. Therefore the object of charity is not a rational nature. The proof of the minor: the precepts of the law are given concerning the acts of the virtues.[8] But there is no precept given that one should love himself. Therefore to love is not an act of charity.

11. Moreover, Gregory says in one of his Homilies,[9] *it is not possible that there be charity between less than two.* Therefore it is not possible for a person to love himself out of charity.

12. Moreover, just as justice consists in a sharing, so does friendship, according to the Philosopher in Book VI of the *Ethic.*[10] But justice, properly speaking, is not of a man toward himself, as is said in Book V of the *Ethic.*[11] Therefore neither is friendship, and neither is charity.

13. Moreover, nothing which is reckoned among the vices is an act of charity. But to love self is considered a vice in man, as is said (II *Tim.* iii. 1), *In the last days, shall come dangerous times. Men shall be lovers of themselves.* Therefore to love self is not an act of charity, and so rational nature is not the proper object of love.

14. Moreover, the human body is a part of rational nature, viz., human nature. But it does not seem that the human body ought to be loved out of charity, since according to the Philosopher in Book IX of the

[7] Aristotle, *Nic. Eth.* IX, 9, 1170b 10; VIII, 5, 1157b 19.
[8] See *Sum. Theol.* I-II, q. 99, a. 2.
[9] See St. Gregory the Great, *Homilarium in Evangelia* I, Hom. XVII; PL 76, 1139.
[10] Aristotle, *Nic. Eth.* V, 1, 1130a 3.
[11] Aristotle, *Nic. Eth.* V, 11, 1138a 12.

Ethic.,[12] those who love themselves for what is exterior to their nature ought to be censured. Therefore rational nature is not the object of love.

15. Moreover, no one who has charity flees from that which he loves out of charity. But the saints having charity flee the body, as is said (*Rom.* vii. 24), *Who shall deliver me from the body of this death?* Thus the body is not to be loved out of charity, and the same argument follows as in the previous objection.

16. Moreover, no one is bound to fulfill that of which he is not capable. But no one can know that he has charity. Therefore no one is bound to love rational creatures out of charity.

17. Moreover, when it is said that a rational creature is loved out of charity, this preposition *out of* designates the relation of a cause of some sort. But it cannot indicate the relation of a material cause, since charity is not something material, but is spiritual.[13] Again, it does not indicate the relation of a final cause, because the end of the one loving out of charity is not charity, but rather it is God.[14] Likewise, neither does it indicate the relation of an efficient cause, because it is the Holy Spirit Who moves us to love, as is said (*Rom.* v. 5), *The charity of God is poured forth in our hearts, by the Holy Ghost, who is given to us.* And again, it does not indicate the relation of a formal cause, because charity is not an intrinsic form since it does not come from the essence of a thing; nor is it the extrinsic exemplary form, for then all things which are loved out of charity would be located in the species of charity, just as imitations are located in the species of the exemplar.[15] Therefore rational creatures are not to be loved out of charity.

18. Moreover, Augustine says in I *De Doctr. Christ.,*[16] that our neighbor is he from whom some favor is received. But we receive favors from God. Therefore God is our neighbor. Thus it was not correctly posited by Augustine that God is one object of love out of charity, neighbor another.[17]

19. Moreover, since Christ is the Mediator between God and man, it seems that He ought to be posited as another object of love, in addition to God and neighbor. There are, therefore, five objects to be loved in charity, and not just four, as Augustine says.[18]

On the contrary, it is said (*Levit.* xix. 18), *Love your neighbor as yourself.* The Gloss is: *Your neighbor is such not only by closeness of*

[12] Aristotle, *Nic. Eth.* IX, 8, 1168b 14.
[13] See *Sum. Theol.* II-II, q. 23, a. 2; q. 27, a. 3.
[14] See *Sum. Theol.* II-II, q. 25, a. 2.
[15] See *Sum. Theol.* II-II, q. 23, a. 8, *ad* 1m.
[16] St. Augustine, *De Doctrina Christiana* I, 30; PL 34, 31.
[17] See St. Augustine, *De Doctr. Christ.* I, 26; PL 34, 29.
[18] See St. Augustine, *De Doctr. Christ.* I, 23; PL 34, 27.

blood-relationship, but also by way of the fellowship of reason. Therefore, according as anything shares with us in the society of rational natures, so it is lovable out of charity. Therefore rational nature is the object of charity.[19]

I answer. It must be said that when there is question of those things which come under the act of any power or habit, the formal notion of the object of that power or habit must be considered.[20] For, it is in terms of their relation to that notion that things come under that power or habit; just as in the case of things visible, it is in terms of their relationship to one and the same notion of being able to be seen, that they are either essentially or accidentally visible.

However, since the object of love taken universally is the good taken commonly, it is necessary that there be some special good as the object of each special love.[21] For example, the proper object of natural friendship, which is friendship toward blood-relatives, is a natural good considered as something produced from parents; in a political friendship, however, the object is the good of the state.[22] Charity, therefore, has a certain special good as its proper object, viz., the good of divine beatitude, as was said above in Article IV of this Question. Thus, according as things are related to this good, so also are they lovable out of charity.

But it should be considered that, since to love is to wish the good of someone, that which is said to be loved has a twofold consideration: it is considered either as one for whom we wish the good; or as the good which we wish for someone.[23]

Therefore, in this first way, only those things can be loved out of charity for which we are able to wish the good of eternal beatitude, for they are the things which were begotten to enjoy a good of this kind.[24] Whence, since only intellectual nature was begotten to enjoy the good of eternal beatitude, then only intellectual nature is to be loved out of charity, according as those things for which we wish this good are said to be loved.

And for this reason, Augustine distinguishes four objects to be loved out of charity according as various things can have eternal beatitude in various ways.[25]

[19] See *Sum. Theol.* II-II, q. 25, a. 3.
[20] See Aristotle, *Nic. Eth.* II, 1, 1103a 31; St. Thomas, *Sum. Theol.* I-II, q. 51, a. 2; q. 54, a. 2; q. 58, a. 3; q. 63, a. 4.
[21] See *Sum. Theol.* II-II, q. 25, a. 12.
[22] See *Sum. Theol.* II-II, q. 26, aa. 2, 7-8.
[23] See Aristotle, *Rhet.* II, 4, 1380b 35; 1381a 19; St. Thomas, *Sum. Theol.* II-II, q. 23, a. 1; q. 27, a. 2.
[24] See *Sum. Theol.* II-II, q. 25, a. 12.
[25] See St. Augustine, *De Doctr. Christ.* I, 23: PL 34, 27. See also St. Thomas, *Sum. Theol.* II-II, q. 25, a. 12.

For, there is that which has eternal beatitude through its own essence, and this is God; and that which has it through participation, and this is the rational creature; both that one that loves, as well as other creatures which can be associated with it in the sharing in beatitude. However, there is something else to which it pertains to have an eternal beatitude, but only through a certain return, viz., our body which is glorified through a redundance of glory from the soul to itself.

Therefore God ought to be loved out of charity as the root of beatitude; however each man ought to love himself in charity in order that he may share in beatitude.[26] He should also love his neighbor as his associate in the participation of beatitude, and his own body according as beatitude redounds to it.[27]

But in the second way, i.e., considered as those goods which we wish for others are said to be loved, everything can be loved out of charity insofar as these are goods of those who are able to enjoy beatitude. For, all creatures are a means for man to tend towards his beatitude, and, further, all creatures are ordered to the glory of God inasmuch as the divine goodness is manifested in them. At this time, therefore, we can love all things out of charity, but only by ordering them to those beings which have, or can have, beatitude.[28]

Now it must also be considered that loves are related to one another in accord with the relation among goods which are their objects. Accordingly, since all human goods are ordered to eternal beatitude as the ultimate end, the love of charity includes within itself all human loves, with the exception of those which are based on sin, which cannot be ordered to beatitude. Whence, that some who are relatives, or fellow-citizens, or fellow pilgrims, or any such, should love *(diligant)* one another, can be meritorious and out of charity;[29] but that some be bound together *(ament se invicem)* for the sake of sharing in robbery or adultery, this cannot be meritorious nor out of charity.

To the first, it must be said that we love virtue and beatitude out of charity inasmuch as we wish them for those for whom it is possible to have beatitude.

To the second, it must be said that God loves all things out of charity, not because He wishes beatitude for them, but He orders these things to Himself and to the other creatures which are able to enjoy beatitude.

[26] See *Sum. Theol.* II-II, q. 25, a. 1.
[27] See *Sum. Theol.* II-II, q. 25, a. 5; q. 26, a. 4.
[28] See *Sum. Theol.* II-II, q. 25, a. 12.
[29] See *Sum. Theol.* II-II, q. 26, a. 8.

To the third, it must be said that all goods are in God as in a first principle. In this way, Origen meant that it is one thing to love God and every other good.[30]

To the fourth, it must be said that all things can be loved meritoriously by ordering them to those which have a capacity for beatitude, not by wishing beatitude for them.

To the fifth, it must be said that there is contained, as a principle, in the good of the universe, rational nature which is capable of beatitude, and to which all other creatures are ordered. According to this, it is fitting both for God and for us to especially love the good of the universe out of charity.

To the sixth, it must be said that, just as charity believes all things that are worthy of belief, so does it love all things according as they are lovable out of charity.

To the seventh, it must be said that we are not able to love God here with that perfection with which we will love Him in our home-land, seeing Him through His essence.[31]

To the eighth, it must be said that the distance separating other creatures is not the reason why they are not loved in charity, but it is because they are not capable of beatitude.[32]

To the ninth, it must be said that angels do not share with us in the life of nature as regards our species, but only as regards the genus of rational nature; but we are able to share with them in the life of glory. As to that which is said (*Matt.* xxv. 15), *To every one He gave according to his proper ability*, this must not be referred only to natural ability, for it is erroneous to say that the gifts of grace and glory are given according to natural measure, but rather here [in this text] must be understood also that ability which is by way of grace, through which it is granted to men that they can merit glory equal to that of the angels.[33]

To the tenth, it must be said that the written law has been given as an aid to the law of nature, which had been obscured by sin.[34] But the law was not rendered so obscure that it would not move one to love, so that man would not love himself or his body; but it was obscured to this extent that it was not moving man to love God and his neighbor. Therefore, in the written law, there had to be given precepts about loving God and neighbor, in which is, nevertheless, also included the precept that

[30] See Origen, *In Cant.* Hom. II; PG 13, 64.
[31] See *Sum. Theol.* II-II, q. 24, a. 8.
[32] See *Sum. Theol.* II-II, q. 25, a. 6.
[33] See *Sum. Theol.* I-II, q. 109, a. 5; q. 110, a. 3; II-II, q. 25, a. 10; *De veritate* q. 27, a. 2.
[34] See *Sum. Theol.* I-II, q. 98, a. 1.

each one love himself.[35] The reason for this is that as we are induced to love God, we are induced to desire Him, by which we especially love ourselves and wish for ourselves the highest good. But in the precept of loving neighbor, it is said, *Love your neighbor as yourself.* In this is included the love of self.[36]

To the eleventh, it must be said that although, properly speaking, friendship cannot be had for self, on the other hand love is had for self. For, it is written in Book IX of the *Ethic.*,[37] that the feelings that constitute friendship for others are an extension of regard for self. But as charity signifies love, thus is one able to love himself in charity. But Gregory speaks of charity considered as it includes the aspect of friendship.[38]

To the twelfth, it must be said that although friendship consists in a sharing with another, just as does justice; love, however, does not necessarily relate to another, which is sufficient for the notion of charity.

To the thirteenth, it must be said that those who love self are censured inasmuch as they love themselves more than they ought. Reproach, indeed, does not pertain to spiritual goods because no one is able to love virtue too much. But one can love himself to excess inasmuch as he loves external and corporeal goods.

To the fourteenth, it must be said that not everyone who loves himself in terms of his exterior nature is at fault, but rather he who seeks exterior goods beyond the measure of virtue. Thus we are able to love our body in charity.[39]

To the fifteenth, it must be said that charity does not flee the body but the corruption of the body, inasmuch as it is said (*Wis.* ix. 15), *For the corruptible body is a load upon the soul.* Because of this the Apostle clearly has said *the body of this death* (*Rom.* vii. 24).

To the sixteenth, it must be said that it does not follow from the fact that man does not know for certain whether he has charity that he is not able to love out of charity,[40] but it does follow that he is not able to judge whether he loves out of charity. Thus, it can be required of us that we love out of charity, but not that we judge that we are loving out of charity. Whence the Apostle says (I *Cor.* iv. 3), *Neither do I judge my own self. . . . but he that judgeth me, is the Lord.*

To the seventeenth, it must be said that when one is said to love his neighbor out of charity, this preposition *out of* can designate a relation

[35] See *Sum. Theol.* I–II, q. 99, a. 5.
[36] See *Sum. Theol.* I–II, q. 100, a. 10.
[37] Aristotle. *Nic. Eth.* IX, 8, 1169a 12.
[38] See St. Gregory the Great. *In Evang.* I, Hom. XVII; PL 76, 1139.
[39] See *Sum Theol.* II–II, q. 25, a. 5.
[40] See *De veritate* q. 10, a. 10.

of final, efficient and formal causes; the final cause inasmuch as the love of neighbor is ordered to the love of God as to an end, whence it is written (I *Tim.* i. 5), *The end of the commandment is charity,* because the love of God is the goal in observing the precepts. In the relationship of efficient cause, however, inasmuch as charity is a habit tending toward loving, being related to the act of loving as heat is to heating. In the relationship of formal cause, however, inasmuch as the act receives its species from the habit, as heating does from heat.

To the eighteenth, it must be said that the notion of being a neighbor is preserved both in him who gives favors and in him who receives, but not that whoever gives favors is a neighbor since it is required among neighbors that there be a sharing in some order. Therefore God, although He gives favors, cannot be said to be our neighbor; but Christ, inasmuch as He is man, is called our neighbor according as He gives favors to us.

From this the answer to the last objection is clear.

ARTICLE VIII

Whether Loving One's Enemies Arises From the Perfection of a Counsel?[1]

It seems that loving one's enemies is not from the perfection of a counsel.

1. That which comes under a precept is not from the perfection of a counsel.[2] But to love one's enemies comes under this precept, viz., *Love your neighbor as yourself,* for by the word *neighbor* is understood all men, as Augustine says in the *De Doctrina Christiana*.[3] Therefore to love one's enemies is not from the perfection of a counsel.

2. But it should be objected that the love of enemies is from the perfection of a counsel, at least to the extent of displaying acquaintance and the other effects of charity. On the contrary, we are bound to love all men in charity. But the love of charity is not only in the heart but also in works, for it is said (I *John* iii. 18), *Let us not love in word, nor in tongue, but in deed, and in truth.* Therefore, considered as the effect of charity, love of enemy comes under a precept.

3. Moreover, it is also written (*Matt.* v. 44), *Love your enemies, do good to them that hate you.* If, therefore, to love your enemy is from a precept, then to do good to him, which pertains to the effect of charity, is also from a precept.

4. Moreover, those things which pertain to the perfection of the counsels were not written in the Old Law, as is said (*Hebr.* vii. 19), *The law brought nothing to perfection.* But in the Old Law, it was taught that not only the affection of love be had for enemies, but also that the effect of love be imparted to them. For, it is written (*Exod.*, xxiii. 4), *If thou meet thy enemy's ox or ass going astray, bring it back to him; (Levit.* xix. 17), *Thou shalt not hate thy brother in thy heart, but reprove him openly, lest thou incur sin through him; (Job* xxxi. 29, 30), *If I have been glad at the downfall of him that hated me, and have rejoiced that evil had found him. For I have not given my mouth to sin; (Prov.* xxv. 21), *If thy enemy be hungry, give him to eat; if he thirst give him water to drink.* Therefore the love of enemies, insofar as it shows the effects of charity, is not from the perfection of a counsel.

5. Moreover, a counsel is not contrary to a precept of the law.[4] For the Lord, when He was about to teach the perfection of the New Law,

---

[1] See *Sum. Theol.* II-II, q. 25, aa. 8-9; *In III Sent.* d. 30, q. 1, a. 1; *De Perf. Vitae Spir.* c. 14; *Ad Rom.* c. 12, l. 13.
[2] See *Sum. Theol.* I-II, q. 108, a. 4; *S.C.G.* III, 130.
[3] St. Augustine, *De Doctr. Christ.* I, 30; PL 34, 31.
[4] See *Sum. Theol.* I-II, q. 108, a. 4; *S.C.G.* III, 130.

first said (*Matt.* v. 17), *I am not come to destroy the law but to fulfill it.* But to love enemies seems to be contrary to the precept of the law, for it is said (*Matt.* v. 43), *Thou shalt love thy neighbor and hate thy enemy.* Therefore the love of enemies does not come under the perfection of a counsel.

6. Moreover, love has its proper object toward which it inclines, as Augustine says, *My weight is my love.*[5] An enemy does not seem to be the proper object of love, but rather he seems to be one resisting love. Therefore it is not of the perfection of charity that an enemy should be loved.

7. Moreover, the perfection of a virtue is not contrary to the inclination of nature; rather, through virtue the inclination of nature is perfected.[6] But it is nature that moves us to hate our enemies, for every natural being rejects its own contrary. Therefore it is not of the perfection of charity that an enemy should be loved.

8. Moreover, the perfection of charity, and of any virtue, consists in our becoming like to God. But God loves His friends and hates His enemies, according to the text (*Malac.* i. 2), *I have loved Jacob, but have hated Esau.* Therefore it is not of the perfection of charity that someone should love his enemies, but rather he should hate them.

9. Moreover, the love of charity looks directly to the good of eternal life. But we ought not to wish the good of eternal life for some of our enemies; for, either they have been condemned to hell, or if they are still living, they have been rejected by God. Therefore to love enemies does not pertain to the perfection of charity.

10. Moreover, we cannot lawfully kill one whom we are bound to love in charity, nor can we wish his death or any other evil for him, because the meaning of friendship is that we wish to be friends and to live. But it is lawful for us to kill some, for, according to the Apostle (*Rom.* xiii. 4), *For he is God's minister: an avenger to execute wrath upon him that doth evil.* Therefore we are not bound to love our enemies.

11. Moreover, the Philosopher in the *Topicorum,*[7] teaches that in the case of contraries the argument runs as follows. If to love your friends and to do good for them is a good thing, then to love your enemies and to do good for them is an evil thing. But no evil attains to the perfection of charity, nor is it included under a counsel. Therefore to love your enemies does not pertain to the perfection of a counsel.

12. Moreover, friend and enemy are contraries. Therefore both to love a friend and to hate an enemy are contraries. But contraries cannot

---

[5] See St. Augustine, *Confessionum* XIII, 9; PL 32, 849.
[6] See *Sum. Theol.* I-II, q. 63, a. 1.
[7] Aristotle, *Topics* II, 7, 112b 1.

exist together. Therefore, since we are bound to love our friends in charity, it cannot be a counsel that we love our enemies.

13. Moreover, a counsel cannot be concerned with the impossible.[8] But to love an enemy seems to be impossible, since it is contrary to the inclination of nature. Therefore to love our enemies is not a counsel.

14. Moreover, to obey the counsels is for the perfect. The Apostles were perfect to a high degree, but they did not love their enemies both with regard to affection and deed. For it was written of St. Thomas the Apostle that he called down upon the one who struck him with an open hand, a curse such that his hand was snatched off by hungry dogs.[9] Therefore to love enemies both as regards affection and deed does not come under the perfection of a counsel.

15. Moreover, to call down evils on anyone, especially the evil of eternal damnation, is opposed to love both as regards affection and deed. But the Prophets called down evils for their adversaries, for it is said *(Psalms* lxviii. 29), *Let them be blotted out of the book of the living; and* with *the just let them not be written.* And again, *(Psalms* liv. 16), *Let death come upon them, and let them go down alive into hell.* Therefore to love enemies does not come under the perfection of charity.

16. Moreover, it is of the very nature of true friendship that someone be loved for his own sake; but charity includes friendship, as the perfect includes the less perfect. But to love one's enemy for his own sake is contrary to charity, for only God is loved for His own sake. Therefore it is not from the perfection of a counsel that our enemy is loved.

17. Moreover, that which is from the perfection of a counsel is better and more meritorious than that which is from the necessity of a precept.[10] But to love an enemy is neither better nor more meritorious than to love a friend, which clearly is from the necessity of a precept; for, if it is good to love something good, it is better and more meritorious to love what is better. But a friend is better than an enemy. Therefore to love an enemy is not from the perfection of a counsel.

18. But it was stated that to love an enemy is more meritorious because it is more difficult. On the contrary, to love an enemy is more difficult than to love God. Therefore, by the same reasoning, it should be more meritorious to love an enemy than to love God.

19. Moreover, a sign that a habit has been formed is pleasure in the work, as the Philosopher writes in Book II of the *Ethic.*[11] But to love a friend is more pleasing than to love an enemy. Therefore it is also more

---

[8] See *Sum. Theol.* I-II, q. 108, a. 4, *ad* 4m.
[9] See *The Acts of Thomas,* I, 6, in *The Apocryphal New Testament,* trans. M. R. James (Oxford, The Clarendon Press, 1955), p. 367.
[10] See *Sum Theol.* I-II, q. 108, a. 4 and *ad* 4m.
[11] Aristotle, *Nic. Eth.* II, 3, 1104b 9.

virtuous, and consequently more meritorious. Thus to love an enemy does not come from the perfection of a counsel.

On the contrary, Augustine writes in the *Enchir.*,[12] that *it is for the perfect sons of God to love their enemies; indeed each one ought to show himself faithful in this love.*

I answer. It must be said that to love one's enemies comes under the necessity of a precept in one way; yet in another way it comes under the perfection of a counsel.

To prove this, it must be known that, as has been said above in Article IV of this Question, the proper and essential object of charity is God; and whatever is loved in charity is loved in terms of that very relationship by which it is related to God.[13] For example, just as if we love some man, we consequently love everything with whom he is concerned, even if they are our own enemies. But it is agreed that all men are related to God as created by Him and as capable of a happiness which consists in the enjoyment of Him. It is clear, therefore, that this meaningful basis of the love that charity involves is found in all men.[14]

Therefore, in one who acts unfriendly toward us, two things are to be considered: one which is the basis of love, viz., in that he is related to God; and another which is the basis of hate, viz., in that he is our adversary. However, if in anyone is found both the basis of love and of hate, and if love is neglected and we turn in the direction of hate, it is clear that the basis of hate predominates in our heart over the basis of love. Thus, therefore, if one regards his enemy with hatred, his enmity toward him predominates in his heart over divine love. Therefore he hates the friendship with such a one more than he loves God. But we hate something to the degree that we love the good of which we are deprived by the enemy. Therefore it remains that whoever hates his enemy loves some created good more than he loves God; and this is against the precept of charity.[15]

But to regard your enemy with hatred is against charity, for it is necessary, if we are bound by the precept of charity, that the love of God predominate in us over the love of any other thing and, as a consequence, also over the hatred of the contrary of that thing. Therefore it follows that we are bound to love our enemies out of the necessity of a precept.[16]

At this point, however, although we are bound by the precept of charity to love our neighbor, the precept does not extend to this that we

---

12 St. Augustine, *Enchiridion* LXXIII; PL 40, 266.
13 See *Sum. Theol.* II-II, q. 26, a. 2.
14 See *Sum. Theol.* II-II, q. 25, a. 8, *ad* 2m.
15 See *Sum. Theol.* II-II, q. 25, a. 8.
16 See *Sum. Theol.* II-II, q. 25, a. 8.

should actually love each and every neighbor in particular or do well by each one in a particular way, because no man is capable of having all men in mind in such a way that he would actually love each one in a particular way, nor is there any one capable of doing good or helping each and every one in a particular way.[17]

But we are bound to love some in a special way and to act for the welfare of those who are joined to us because of some other bond of friendship, for all other lawful loves are included under charity, as was said above.[18] Whence Augustine says, *You cannot do good to all men, you are to pay special regard to those who, by the accidents of time, or place, or circumstance, are brought into closer connection with you. . . . You must take the matter as decided for you by a sort of lot, according as each man happens for the time being to be more closely connected with you.*[19]

From this it is clear that we are not bound by the precept of charity to be moved by the affection of love or by the carrying out of the works of charity in a special way towards him who is not united to us by any other bond, except to him united to us by the chance bond of location or of time, and especially if we would see him in some necessity through which he would not be able to be helped except by us. We are bound, however, by the affection and the carrying out of the works of charity, by which we love all our neighbors and pray for them, not to exclude even those who are not joined to us by any special bond, as for instance those who live in India or Ethiopia.[20]

When no other bond remains to join us to our enemies except the bond of charity, we are bound by the obligation of precept to love them in common, both with affection and deed, and individually when the moment of need threatens.[21] But when man for the sake of God shows toward his enemies that special affection and deeds of love which he devotes to those who are joined to him, this is perfect charity and follows from a counsel.[22] For, it arises from the perfection of charity that charity alone should so move one toward an enemy in the manner that both charity and particular love move one toward a friend.

It is evident, however, that the fact that the action of an agent attains to that which is distant is due to the perfection of its active power. For the power of fire is more perfect when not only things nearby but also those distant are heated. So also that charity is more perfect through

[17] See *Sum. Theol.* II-II, q. 25, a. 9; q. 44, a. 1.
[18] Article IV of this Question.
[19] See St. Augustine, *De Doctr. Christ.* I, 28; PL 34, 30.
[20] See *Sum. Theol.* II-II, q. 26, a. 7; q. 44, aa. 2-3.
[21] See Aristotle, *Nic. Eth.* IX, 3, 1165b 13.
[22] See *Sum. Theol.* II-II, q. 25, a. 6.

which one is moved, both in loving and in doing good, toward not only neighbors but also foreigners, and beyond this even to enemies, not only in general but in particular.

To the first, it must be said that the love of enemies is contained in a precept, as has been said.[23]

To the second, it must be said that we ought to love our enemies, just as much in deed as in affection, as has been said.[24]

The answer to the third objection can be seen from the above.

To the fourth, it must be said that those authorities of the Old Testament speak of the case of necessity when we are bound by a precept to do good to our enemies, as has been said in the body of the Article. ·

To the fifth, it must be said that what is written, *Hate your enemy,* is not found in the entire Old Testament, but this is from the tradition of the Scribes to whom it seemed that it should be added because the Lord commanded the sons of Israel to persecute their enemies. It should also be said that this saying, *Hate your enemy,* should not be interpreted as an order to the just but as a permission to the weak, as Augustine says in the *De Sermone Domini in Monte.*[25] Or, as Augustine also writes in the *Contra Faustum,*[26] men ought not to hate their enemy but only vice.

To the sixth, it must be said that one's enemy, considered as enemy, is not the object of love but is so only insofar as he pertains to God. Therefore we ought to hate in our enemy the fact that he hates us, and to desire that he would love us.

To the seventh, it must be said that man, by nature, loves all men, as the Philosopher says in Book VIII of the *Ethic.*[27] But that one becomes an enemy is from something that is superadded to nature, and, accordingly, the inclination of nature ought not to be taken away. Therefore charity, when it moves to the love of enemies, perfects the natural inclination; the case is otherwise in things which are natural contraries, such as fire and water, or wolf and lamb.

To the eighth, it must be said that God does not hate anything that is His own, such as the natural good or any other thing; but He only hates what is not His, viz., sin. And so also we ought to love in men that which is of God, and to hate what is foreign to God, according as it is said (*Psalms* cxxxviii. 22), *I have hated them with a perfect hatred.*

To the ninth, it must be said that we ought not to wish those who are known to be damned to have eternal life, because they are already wholly excluded from this by the divine decree; but we can love them

---

[23] See the Reply to this Article.
[24] See the Reply to this Article.
[25] St. Augustine, *De Sermone Domini in Monte* I, 21; PL 34, 1265.
[26] St. Augustine, *Contra Faustum* XXIX, 24; PL 42, 362
[27] Aristotle, *Nic. Eth.* VIII, 1, 1155a 6.

[71]

as works of God in which the divine justice is manifested. In this manner does God love them. But we ought to wish those who are not yet known to be damned to have life eternal. This foreknowledge is not given to us, and the foreknowledge of God does not exclude the possibility of their attaining eternal life.

To the tenth, it must be said that he whose office prescribes it, may lawfully punish evil-doers or even kill them while loving them out of charity. For, Gregory says in one of his Homilies that the just, while still loving, may cause a persecution; for if outwardly they create unrest by disciplining, inwardly, however, they may preserve their serenity by charity.[28]

Now we can desire or cause some temporal evil for those whom we love in charity for three reasons: first, we can do it in order to correct them; secondly, it may be because the temporal prosperity of some is detrimental to the good of some multitude or even the whole Church, whence Gregory writes in XXII *Moral.*,[29] *It often happens that the ruin of our enemy can make us happy without our losing charity, and again, his glory can sadden us without incurring the fault of envy. This happens when, by his downfall, we believe that some are profited more, or when, by his advantage, we fear that many will be unjustly oppressed.* Thirdly, our motive may be in order to preserve the order of divine justice, according as it is written (*Psalms* lvii. 11), *The just shall rejoice when he shall see the revenge.*

To the eleventh, it must be said that propositions of this kind, by which the Philosopher argues,[30] are to be taken as evident in themselves. For, just as it is good to love a friend insofar as he is a friend, so it is evil to love an enemy because he is an enemy. But it is good to love an enemy insofar as he pertains to God.

To the twelfth, it must be answered that to love a friend as friend and an enemy as enemy are contraries. But to love a friend and an enemy insofar as they both belong to God is not contrary; just as it is not contrary to see white and to see black when both are considered as colored.

To the thirteenth, it must be said that to love an enemy as enemy is difficult, even impossible. But to love an enemy because of some greater love is easy. That is why the love of God makes easy that which seems to be impossible in itself.

To the fourteenth, it must be said that St. Thomas did not ask for

---

[28] See St. Gregory the Great, *Epistalorum* XLVIII; PL 77, 511-512; *Regulae Pastoralis* III, 30; PL 77, 110-112.
[29] St. Gregory the Great, *Moralium XXII*, 11; PL 75, 226.
[30] See Aristotle, *Topics*, II, 7, 112b 1.

the punishment of his assailant because of a desire for revenge, but as a manifestation of the divine justice and power.[31]

To the fifteenth, it must be said that these pleas which are found in the Prophets should be understood as predictions, so that *let them be blotted out (deleantur)* means *they will be blotted out (delebuntur)*. For, they used such a manner of speaking because they were conforming their own wills to the divine justice revealed to them.

To the sixteenth, it must be said that to love one for his own sake can be understood in two ways. First, in such a way that one is loved as a final end; and thus only God should be loved for His own sake. Secondly, that we love him for whom we wish some good, as is proper to a friendship for a noble person; but not as the good which we wish for ourselves, as is proper to a friendship for a pleasant or useful person, in which we love a friend as our own good. For, it is not that we seek pleasure or utility for a friend, but that we seek pleasure or utility for ourselves from a friend; just as we also love things pleasing and useful for ourselves, such as food or clothing. But when we love one out of virtue, we wish good for him, and we do not wish him for ourselves; this is especially proper to the friendship of charity.

To the seventeenth, it must be said that it is better to love an enemy than to love only a friend,[32] because this shows more perfect charity, as was said above in the body of the Article. But if we consider these two absolutely, it is better to love a friend than an enemy; it is also better to love God than a friend. For, the difficulty which is found in loving an enemy does not constitute the reason for meriting, except insofar as perfect charity is demonstrated by it, which overcomes the difficulty. Thus, if there would be such a perfect charity as to take away all difficulty, to this extent it would be more meritorious. But we speak of one who loves a friend with such perfect charity that it even extends to the love of enemies; but this love operates with more ardor toward the friend, unless by chance it is considered accidentally insofar as it operates against something repugnant with a greater effort. For example, in natural things, water that is warm is with greater effort brought to the freezing point.

The answer to the eighteenth and nineteenth objections is clear from what was just stated.

[31] See *Acts of Thomas, op. cit.* p. 367.
[32] See *Sum. Theol.* II-II, q. 27, a. 7.

[73]

ARTICLE IX

Whether There Is Some Order In Charity?[1]

It seems that there is no order in charity.

1. For, just as faith involves what is believed, so charity involves what should be loved. But faith equally believes all things which should be believed. Therefore charity equally loves all things which should be loved.[2]

2. Moreover, order pertains to the intellect.[3] But charity is not in the intellect, for it is in the will.[4] Therefore order does not pertain to charity.

3. Moreover, wherever there is order, there are various gradations. But according to Bernard, *Charity does not know any hierarchy, nor does it consider any dignity.*[5] Therefore there is no order in charity.

4. Moreover, the object of charity is God, as Augustine says in the *De Doctr. Christ.,*[6] for charity loves nothing except God in fellow-men. But God is not greater in Himself than in fellow-men, nor is He greater in one brother than in another. Therefore charity does not love God more than neighbor, nor does it love one neighbor more than another.

5. Moreover, a similitude is the principle of love, according as it is written *(Ecclus. xiii. 19), Every beast loveth its like.* But there is a greater likeness of man to his neighbor than there is of man to God. Therefore there is no order in charity in the way Ambrose says that God is loved first.[7]

6. Moreover, it is said (I *John* iv. 20), *He that loveth not his brother, whom he seeth, how can he love God, whom he seeth not?* But St. John argues by a negation from the love of neighbor to the love of God. A negative argument, however, is not taken from the minor premise, but from the major. Therefore neighbor ought to be loved more than God.

7. Moreover, love is a unitive force, as Dionysius says.[8] But nothing is more one to a person than he himself. Therefore man ought not to love God more than himself in charity.

8. Moreover, Augustine says in I *De Doctrina Christ.,*[9] that all men

---

[1] See *Sum. Theol.* II-II, q. 26, a. 1; *In III Sent.* d. 29, q. 1, a. 1.
[2] See *Sum. Theol.* I-II, q. 62, a. 3; II-II, q. 23, a. 6; q. 25, a. 1; *De veritate*, q. 14, a. 5; *De Virt. in Comm.* aa. 10 and 11.
[3] See *Sum. Theol.* I, q. 82, a. 4 and *ad* 1m.
[4] See *Sum. Theol.* II-II, q. 24, a. 1.
[5] See St. Bernard, *Sermones in Cantica Canticorum* LXXIX; PL 183, 1165-1166.
[6] St. Augustine, *De Doctr. Christ.* I, 27; PL 34, 29.
[7] See Origen, *In Cant.* Hom. II; PG 13, 64.
[8] See Dionysius, *De Divinis Nominibus* IV; PG 3, 709.
[9] St. Augustine, *De Doctr. Christ.* I, 28; PL 34, 30.

are to be loved equally. Therefore one neighbor ought not to be loved more than another.

9. Moreover, it is commanded that one love his neighbor as himself. Therefore all fellow-men should be loved equally.

10. Moreover, we have greater love for him to whom we wish the greater good. But in charity we wish one good for all our neighbors, i.e., eternal life. Therefore we ought not to love one neighbor more than another.

11. Moreover, if order is a condition of charity, the order of charity would then fall under one of the precepts. But it does not seem that order is from a precept, because whenever we love one whom we ought to love, it does not seem to be a sin to love another even more. Therefore order is not a condition of charity.

12. Moreover, the charity of this life is in imitation of the charity of heaven. But in heaven, those who are better are loved more; not necessarily those who are closer to us.[10] Therefore it seems that if there is any order in charity, then those who lead better lives here, not those who are closer to us, ought to be loved more. This is contrary to Ambrose who says that God ought to be loved first, then parents, then children, and finally the rest of the domestic household.[11]

13. Moreover, the reason for loving someone in charity is God. But sometimes those who are not close to us are united with God more than our relatives or even our parents.[12] Therefore they ought to be loved more in charity.

14. Moreover, as Gregory writes in one of his Homilies, the proof of love is a demonstration in works.[13] But sometimes the effect of love, which is doing good, is shown more toward those who are not close to us rather than it is to our neighbors; as is clear in the case of the collection for ecclesiastical benefices. Therefore it does not seem that those close to us ought to be loved more in charity.

15. Moreover, it is said (I *John* iii. 18), *Let us not love in word, nor in tongue, but in deed, and in truth.* But sometimes we show more of the deeds of love to others than we do to our parents; e.g., a soldier obeys the general of the army more than he does his father, and one ought to give more to a benefactor than to his father if they are both in equal necessity.[14] Therefore parents ought not to be loved more.

16. Moreover, Gregory says that those whom we receive from the sacred fountain ought to be loved more by us than those who are born

[10] See *Sum. Theol.* II-II, q. 26, a. 7, 13.
[11] See Origen, *In Cant.* Hom. II; PG 13, 64.
[12] See *Sum. Theol.* II-II, q. 26, a. 8.
[13] See St. Gregory the Great, *In Evang.* II, Hom. 30; PL 76, 1220.
[14] See *Sum. Theol.* II-II, q. 26, aa. 8, 12.

[75]

to our flesh.[15] Therefore those who are not members of one's family are to be loved more than those who are close to us.

17. Moreover, he ought to be loved more whose friendship is broken off with more blame. But it seems that the friendship of those friends whom we freely choose is more culpably broken off than that of our relatives who are given to us, not of our own choice, but by a chance of nature. Therefore other friends ought to be loved more than our own relatives.[16]

18. Moreover, if by reason of a closer proximity one should be loved more, then since a wife who is one in flesh is closer, or children who are a part of the parent are closer than the parents are, it seems that children or a wife ought to be loved more than parents.[17] Therefore parents should not be loved most. Thus there does not seem to be that order in charity which is designated by the saints.

On the contrary, it is said *(Cant.* ii. 4), *The king brought me into the cellar of wine, he set in order charity in me.*

I answer. It must be said that, according to every opinion or authority on Scripture, such order must, without doubt, be designated to charity so that God is loved above all things, both in regard to affection and to the effect of love.

However, concerning the love for fellow-men, it was the opinion of some that the order of charity had to do with the effects of love, and not with the loving itself; and they were influenced by the words of Augustine, who writes that all men ought to be loved equally, but *since you cannot do good to all, you are to pay special regard to those who, by the accidents of time, or place, or circumstance, are brought into closer connection with you.*[18]

But this seems to be an unreasonable position, for God so provides for each man according as his state in life requires. Thus love and a desire for the end are implanted by God in those things which tend toward the end of their nature, according as each one's individual state demands that it tend toward its end. Therefore in these things there is a stronger movement according to nature toward a certain end, and there is also in them a greater inclination, which is the natural appetite; as can be seen in heavy and light objects. But, just as the appetite or natural love is a certain inclination implanted in natural things to ends which are connatural to them, so the love of charity is a certain inclination infused in rational nature for the purpose of tending toward God. Therefore,

[15] See St. Gregory the Great, *Moral.* XLVIII, 43; PL 76, 91.
[16] See *Sum. Theol.* II-II, q. 26, a. 8.
[17] See *Sum. Theol.* II-II, q. 26, aa. 11-12.
[18] See St. Augustine, *De Doctr. Christ.* I, 28; PL 34, 30.

according as it is necessary for one to tend toward God, thus is he inclined out of charity.[19]

However, for those who will tend toward God as to an end, what is especially needed is that there be divine help; secondly, that there be some self-help; and thirdly, that there be cooperation with fellow-men. And in this we see a gradation, for some cooperate only in a general way, while others who are more closely united cooperate in a special way. Not all are able to cooperate in a special way. Our body and those things which are necessary for the body also help us tend toward God, but only instrumentally.[20]

Thus it is necessary that the affection of man be so inclined through charity that, first and foremost, each one loves God; secondly, that he love himself; and thirdly, that he love his neighbor. And among the fellow-men, he ought to give mutual help to those who are more closely united to him or who are more closely related to him.[21]

But whoever there is that is a hindrance to this love, should be hated, for the Lord said *(Luke* xiv. 26), *If any man come to me, and hate not his father, and mother, . . . he cannot be my disciple.* Finally, we ought to love our body.[22] Thus, regarding the act which charity evokes, an order ought to be established according to the affection in the love of fellow-men.

However, it should also be considered that, as we said above in Article VII and VIII, other lawful and noble loves which arise from other causes are also able to be ordered to charity. Thus, the charity of these loves can command an act; and therefore that which is loved more according to some of these loves is loved more out of that charity which commands the act. It is also clear that, according to natural love, our relatives are more loved in affection; according to a social love, those who are closely united to us are loved more; and so for all the other kinds of love.[23]

Therefore it is also evident that in affection, one neighbor ought to be loved more than another; and he is loved out of a charity which commands the act of the other lawful friendships.

To the first, it must be said that the object of faith is the true, whence according as something happens to be more true, so is it more believed. But since truth consists in the conformity of intellect and thing, and if truth is considered according to the characteristic of equality which does not allow a greater or less degree, it does not then happen that a thing is more or less true. But if the being itself of the thing is considered,

---

[19] See the Reply to Article I of this Question.
[20] See *Sum. Theol.* II-II, q. 26, aa. 5, 7; q. 27, a. 6.
[21] See *Sum. Theol.* II-II, q. 26, aa. 2, 7.
[22] See *Sum. Theol.* II-II, q. 26, a. 5.
[23] See Aristotle, *Nic. Eth.* IX, 2, 1165a 17; St. Thomas, *Sum. Theol.* II-II, q. 26, a. 8.

[77]

which is the basis of truth, as is said in II *Metaphys.*,[24] then the disposition of things in being and in truth is the same. Thus, those things which are more in being are more true, and because of this, principles in scientific demonstrations are believed more than conclusions. And thus it happens also in regard to those things which concern faith. In this way the Apostle (I *Cor.* xv) proves the future resurrection of the dead through the resurrection of Christ.

To the second, it must be said that the order of reason is as that which orders, but the order of the will is as that which is ordered.[25] Therefore order is proper to charity.

To the third, it must be said that charity does not recognize a hierarchy of the lover to the loved because it unites the two. It does, however, recognize the hierarchy of two objects to be loved.

To the fourth, it must be said that although God is not greater in one than in another, however He is more perfectly in Himself than in creatures, and in one creature than in another.

To the fifth, it must be said that in the love whose principal object is the one loving, it is necessary that what is more similar to the one loving be loved more, as in a natural love. But in the love of charity, the principal object is God Himself. Thus other things being equal, that which is more one with God ought to be loved more out of charity.

To the sixth, it must be said that the Apostle (I *John* iv. 20) was arguing according to those who are attached in a great degree to what is visible, and by these men, what can be seen is loved more than what cannot be seen.

To the seventh, it must be said that by a unity of nature nothing is more one than we ourselves. But by a unity of affection, whose object is the good, the highest good ought to be more one than we are.

To the eighth, it must be said that all men ought to be loved equally insofar as we ought to wish for all of them the same good, viz., eternal life.[26]

To the ninth, it must be said that one is bound to love his neighbor as himself, but not however as much as himself. Because of this, it does not follow that all fellow-men ought to be loved equally.

To the tenth, it must be said that we speak of loving someone more not only because we wish a greater good for him, but also because we wish the same good for him with more intense affection. Thus, although we wish the one good, which is eternal life, for all; we do not, however, love all equally.

[24] Aristotle, *Metaph.* II (a), 1, 993b 30.
[25] See *Sum. Theol.* I, q. 82, a. 4, *ad* 1m.
[26] See St. Augustine, *De Doctr. Christ.* I, 28; PL 34, 30.

To the eleventh, it must be answered that we are not giving to a person that love which we ought to give if we love more one whom we ought to love less. For, it can happen that in the moment of necessity we give more to the latter, to the neglect of the former whom we ought to love more.

To the twelfth, it must be said that those who are in heaven are joined to their final end, and therefore their love is regulated solely by that end; thus there is no order of charity in them, except that which is concerned with their nearness to God. Because of this, those who are closer to God are loved more. But in this life, it is necessary for us to tend toward our end; and therefore the order of love is also established according to the measure of help in tending to that end which is obtained from others. And thus it is not always those who live better lives that are loved more, but there also arises a factor of propinquity, so that the reason for greater love is found jointly in each of these factors.[27]

From this the answer to the thirteenth objection is also evident.

To the fourteenth, it must be said that any prelate of the Church does not confer benefices insofar as he is Peter or Martin, but only insofar as he is a master of the Church. Therefore, in the collection for ecclesiastical benefices he ought not to regard any closeness to himself but rather the closeness to God and the usefulness to the Church; just as the overseer of any household in attending to the affairs of his master ought to consider the service as being rendered to his master and not to himself. But in one's own private affairs, such as the goods of patrimony, or those things which are acquired by one's own personal effort as an individual, in these goods one ought to observe an order of closeness in doing good.

To the fifteenth, it must be said that concerning those things which properly pertain to the individual person of anyone, he ought to show more of the effects of love towards his parents than toward someone who is not a member of his family; except if by chance, when the common good which each one ought also to desire for himself would depend on the good of someone who is not a member of one's family, as when one would expose himself to the danger of death in order to save the general of the army in war time, or to save the leader of a state insofar as the welfare of the entire community depends on these men. But considering those things which pertain to some other thing by reason of a certain bond, such as the fact that one is a citizen or a soldier, he ought to obey the ruler of the state or his general more than his parents.[28]

27 See *Sum. Theol.* II-II, q. 26, aa. 7, 13.
28 See *Sum. Theol.* II-II, q. 26, aa. 8, 12.

To the sixteenth, it must be said that when we refer to those whom we receive from the sacred fountain, the text of Gregory ought to be understood as meaning that which pertains to a spiritual regeneration.[29]

To the seventeenth, it must be said that this argument applies only to those things which pertain to our social life, in which is founded friendship for someone who is not a member of one's family.

To the eighteenth, it must be said that according to that love by which one loves himself, he loves his wife and children more than his parents because a wife is some part of the husband, and the son of the father. Therefore the love which one has for his wife and son is more included in the love by which a person loves himself than is the love which he has for his parents. But this is not to love the son for the son's sake, but rather for one's own sake.[30]

But according to the mode of love by which we love another for the other's sake, a father ought to be loved more than a son insofar as we receive greater benefit from the father, and also insofar as the honor of the son depends more on the honor of the father than vice versa. Therefore in a display of reverence, in obedience, in doing the will of another, and in other similar things, man is bound more to his father than to his son. But in providing the necessities, he is bound more to the child than to the parent,[31] because parents ought to lay away treasures for their children and not vice versa, as is said in I *Corinth.,* iv.[32]

[29] See St. Gregory the Great. *Moral.* XLVIII, 43; PL 76, 91.
[30] See *Sum. Theol.* II-II, q. 26, aa. 11-12.
[31] See *Sum. Theol.* II-II, q. 26, aa. 11-12.
[32] See II *Cor.* xii. 14.

ARTICLE X

Whether Charity Can Be Perfect In This Life?[1]

It seems that charity can be perfect in this life.

1. God commands nothing impossible for man, as Jerome says.[2] But perfect charity is placed in a precept, as is shown *(Deut.* vi. 5), *Love the Lord thy God with thy whole heart;* for *whole* and *perfect* mean the same thing. Therefore it is possible for charity to be perfect in this life.

2. Moreover, Augustine says that this is perfect charity, that better things be loved more.[3] But this is possible in this life. Therefore charity can be perfect in this life.

3. Moreover, the essence of love implies a certain union. But charity is especially able to be one in this life, for it is said (I *Cor.* vi. 17), *He who is joined to the Lord is one spirit.* Therefore charity can be perfect in this life.

4. Moreover, something is perfect which is farthest removed from its contrary. But charity in this life is able to resist every sin and temptation.[4] Therefore charity is able to be perfect in this life.

5. Moreover, our affective power in this life is directed to God immediately through love. But when the intellect is directed immediately to God, we will know Him perfectly and completely.[5] Therefore we love God perfectly and completely now, and so charity is perfect in this life.

6. Moreover, the will is the mistress of its acts. But to love God is an act of the will.[6] Therefore the human will can be completely and perfectly directed to God.

7. Moreover, the object of charity is the divine goodness which is most lovable. But it is not difficult to adhere closely and without ceasing to that which is lovable. Therefore it seems that the perfection of charity can easily be had in this life.

8. Moreover, that which is simple and indivisible, if it is possessed in any manner at all, is possessed completely. But the love of charity is simple and indivisible, both on the part of the soul loving and on the part of the object to be loved, which is God.[7] Therefore, if one has charity in this life, he has it completely and perfectly.

---

[1] See *Sum. Theol.* II-II, q. 24, a. 8; q. 184, a. 2; *In III Sent.* d. 27, q. 3, a. 4; *De Perf. Vit. Spir.* c. III; *Ad Philipp* c. III.

[2] See St. Jerome, *In Evangelium Matthaei* I; PL 26, 42.

[3] See St. Augustine, *De Vera Religione* XLVII; PL 34, 164.

[4] See *Sum. Theol.* II-II, q. 24, a. 9.

[5] See *Sum. Theol.* II-II, q. 27, a. 4.

[6] See *Sum. Theol.* II-II, q. 24, a. 1.

[7] See *Sum. Theol.* II-II, q. 27, a. 5; q. 184, a. 2.

9. Moreover, charity is the most noble of the virtues, according to what is written (I *Cor.* xii. 31), *I shew unto you yet a more excellent way,* i.e., the way of charity. But the other virtues can be perfect in this life. Therefore so also can charity.

On the contrary, (1) since every sin is repugnant to charity, as has been said,[8] the perfection of charity requires that a man be entirely free from sin. But this is not possible in this life, according as it is written (I *John* i. 8), *If we say that we have no sin, we deceive ourselves.* Therefore perfect charity cannot be had in this life.

(2) Moreover, nothing is loved unless it is known, as Augustine says in the *De Trinit.*[9] But in this life God cannot be known perfectly, as is said (I *Cor.* xiii. 9), *For we know in part.* Therefore neither can He be loved perfectly.

(3) Moreover, that which is always able to grow is not perfect. But charity can always grow in this life, as is taught.[10] Therefore charity is not always able to be perfect in this life.

(4) Moreover, *perfect charity casteth out fear,* as is said (I *John* iv. 18). But in this life man cannot be without fear.[11] Therefore no one is able to have perfect charity.

I answer. It must be said that the perfect is spoken of in three ways: first, the perfect in itself; secondly, the perfect according to nature; and thirdly, the perfect according to time. A thing is called perfect in itself when it is perfect in every respect and when no perfection is lacking. Something is called perfect according to nature when it lacks none of the things which it should possess by its very nature. For example, we say that the intellect of man is perfect, not because it lacks none of the intelligibles, but rather because it lacks none of those things through which man naturally knows. We say a thing is perfect according to time when nothing is lacking to it of those things which it is born to have according to a particular time, as we call a boy perfect because he possesses everything that is required for a human being of that age.

So it must be said that charity which is perfect without any qualification is possessed by God alone. But charity which is perfect according to nature can be had by man, but not in this life. Charity which is perfect according to time can be had even in this life.[12]

To understand this clearly, it should be known that since act and habit are specified by their object, it is necessary that any reason of

[8] See Article VI.

[9] St. Augustine, *De Trinit.* X, 1, 2; PL 42, 973, 975.

[10] See St. Augustine, *Tract. in Joan.* LXXIV; PL 35, 1827. See also St. Thomas, *Sum. Theol.* II-II, q. 24, aa. 4-7.

[11] See *Sum. Theol.* I-II, q. 42, a. 3; II-II, q. 19, aa. 2, 10.

[12] See *Sum. Theol.* II-II, q. 24, a. 8; q. 27, a. 5; q. 44, a. 6.

their perfection arise from this same object. But the object of charity is the highest good. Therefore charity is perfect without qualification not only when it is directed to the highest good, but in the same degree as that good is good. Therefore since the highest good is infinite, it is to be loved infinitely. Whence no created charity, since it is finite, can be perfect without qualification, but only the love of God by which He loves Himself can be called perfect in this way.[13]

However, according to the nature of a rational creature, charity is said to be perfect when the rational creature is turned to loving God as much as he is able to love Him. But man is impeded in this life, so that his mind is not directed completely to God, for three reasons. The first reason is the contrary inclination of the soul, for when the soul is turned by sin toward a changeable good as toward an end, it is directed away from the immutable good. Secondly, man does not completely love God because of his occupation with the affairs of the world; for, as the Apostle says (I *Cor.* vii. 33), *He that is with a wife, is solicitous for the things of the world, how he may please his wife; and he is divided;* i.e., his heart is not directed only to God. The third reason is from the infirmity of this present life, with the necessities with which man must be occupied to a certain extent, and his soul must be diverted from being directed to God perfectly, e.g., sleeping, eating, and doing other things of this kind without which the present life could not be lived. Further, the soul is weighted down by the burden of the body so that it cannot see the divine light in its essence.[14] By such a vision, charity would be perfected, according as the Apostle says (II *Cor.* v. 6-7), *While we are in the body, we are absent from the Lord. (For we walk by faith, and not by sight.)*

However, man can live in this life without turning himself away from God by mortal sin. Again, he is able to live without the occupation of temporal affairs, as is said (I *Cor.* vii. 32), *He that is without a wife, is solicitous for the things that belong to the Lord, how he may please God.* However, man cannot be free from the burden of his corruptible body in this life.

Thus, according as the first two impediments are removed, charity can be perfect in this life; but not as regards the third. Therefore no one can possess in this life the perfect charity he will have in the next life, unless he be at one and the same time a traveler here below and a beholder of God, and this is proper only to Christ.

To the first, it must be said that when it is written, *Love the Lord thy God with thy whole heart,* this is understood to be a precept accord-

[13] See *Sum. Theol.* II-II, q. 24, a. 8; q. 27, a. 5; q. 44, a. 6.
[14] See p. 13, n. 38.

ing to which the totality excludes everything that prevents a perfect adherence to God; and this is not a precept but the end of a precept. For us this does not mean that we should do it, but rather that we should tend toward it, as Augustine says.[15]

To the second, it must be said that man is not able to love better things more than their goodness demands; just as he is not able to have perfect charity, as has been said.[16]

To the third, it must be said that in the union which makes the lover one with the loved, there are various grades found. Our soul will then be one with God perfectly when it is always actually directed toward Him, which is not possible in this life.

To the fourth, it must be answered that the perfection which is found in a thing according to its species is found in it always; just as man, because of his rational soul, is perfect at any time or at any age. Whence, the perfection of charity which is according to all time is the perfection which is found in charity according to its species. But it is of the very essence of charity that God be loved above all things and that no creature be preferred to Him in love. Whence, since every temptation occurs from the love of some created good, or from the fear of a contrary evil which is derived from love, charity, in whatever degree, has from its species that it is able to resist any temptation in such way that man is not led into mortal sin through it,[17] not however that man is affected in no way by temptation; for this pertains to the perfection of heaven.

To the fifth, it must be said that in heaven God will be both wholly seen and wholly loved in the same way, viz., insofar as *wholly* is regarded on the part of the one who loves and the one who sees, for the entire power of the creature will be applied to seeing and loving God.[18] Likewise, it can also be understood that God will be wholly seen and loved because there is no part of Him which is not seen and loved, since He is not composite but simple. But according to another way of understanding this, He is not wholly loved or seen, because He will not be seen or loved by any creature to the degree that He can be seen or is lovable.[19]

In this life, however, God cannot even be wholly seen or loved according to the first or second way, for He is not seen through His essence, nor is it possible for man living in this life that his affective power

---

[15] See St. Augustine, *De Moribus Ecclesiae* VIII; PL 32, 1316.
[16] See the Reply to this Article.
[17] See *Sum. Theol.* II-II, q. 24, a. 9; q. 44, a. 4.
[18] See *Sum. Theol.* II-II, q. 27, a. 5.
[19] See *Sum. Theol.* II-II, q. 27, a. 5.

be perfectly directed toward God without any interruption. Nevertheless, God is wholly loved in some way by man in this life according as there is nothing in his affective power contrary to the divine love.[20]

To the sixth, it must be said that the will is the mistress of its own act in regard to that which it does, but not in regard to the fact that it perseveres continually in one act, since a condition of this life requires that acts and the will be directed toward many things. Or, it can be said that the will is the mistress of its acts in those things which are connatural to man, but the perfection of charity which will be greatest in heaven is above man, especially if man is considered according to his state in the present life.[21]

To the seventh, it must be said that an action can cease to be lovable not only on the part of the object, but also on the part of the agent because he is deficient in the power of acting. Thus it must be said that what is always actually directed toward God is lovable on the part of the object. However, such a love, on the part of one living in this life, cannot be continual, because the contemplation of the human mind is not without the action of the imaginative power and of the other corporeal powers, which must be released from continuous action because of the weakness of the body; and for this reason delight is impeded. Thus it is written (Eccle. xii. 1), *Much study is an affliction of the flesh.*

To the eighth, it must be said that the perfection of charity is not according to a quantitative increase, but according to a qualitative intensity. This intensity is not opposed to the simplicity of charity.[22]

To the ninth, it must be said that the objects of the other moral virtues are human goods which do not exceed the powers of man. Therefore man can arrive at the complete perfection of these in this life.[23] But the object of charity is the uncreated good which does exceed the powers of man.[24] Therefore the argument does not apply.

To the first objection given in the On the contrary, it must be said that a man can live in this life without mortal sin, but not without venial sin; this is not contrary to the perfection of this life but to the perfection of the life in heaven which consists in being always actually directed toward God. Venial sin does not take away the habit of charity, but it impedes its act.[25]

To the second, it must be said that we are not able to know God perfectly in this life so that we know what He is. However, we can know

[20] See *Sum. Theol.* II-II, q. 27, a. 5.
[21] See *Sum. Theol.* II-II, q. 23, a. 2.
[22] See *Sum. Theol.* II-II, q. 24, a. 4.
[23] See *Sum. Theol.* I-II, q. 60, a. 5.
[24] See *Sum. Theol.* II-II, q. 24, a. 2.
[25] See *Sum. Theol.* II-II, q. 24, a. 10; q. 44, a. 4, *ad* 2m.

what He is not, as Augustine says,[26] and in this consists the perfection of the knowledge of this life. Likewise, we are not able to love God perfectly in this life so that we are always actually directed toward Him, but the mind is never directed to what is contrary to God.[27]

To the third, it must be said that in this life charity is neither perfect without qualification nor according to human nature, but only according to time.[28] But those things which are perfect in this way possess that by which they grow, as is clear in the example given of boys.[29] Therefore charity in this life always has that by which it increases itself.

To the fourth, it must be said that perfect charity drives out servile and initial fear, but not a chaste or filial fear, or even a natural fear.[30]

[26] See St. Augustine, *De Trinit.* VIII, 2; PL 42, 947.
[27] See *Sum. Theol.* II-II, q. 24, a. 8.
[28] See the Reply to this Article.
[29] See *Sum. Theol.* II-II, q. 24, a. 9.
[30] See *Sum. Theol.* II-II, q. 19, a. 6; q. 19, aa. 8-9.

ARTICLE XI

Whether All Are Bound to Perfect Charity?[1]

It seems that all are bound to perfect charity.

1. All are bound to that which is commanded by a precept. But the perfection of charity is in a precept, for it is said (*Deut.* vi. 5), *Love the Lord thy God with thy whole heart.* Therefore all are bound to the perfection of charity.

2. Moreover, it seems to be from the perfection of charity that man orders all of his acts to God. But all men are bound to do this, for it is written (I *Cor.* x. 31), *Whether you eat or drink, or whatsoever else you do, do all to the glory of God.* Therefore all are bound to the perfection of charity.

3. But it must be objected that this precept of the Apostle means that everything should be ordered to God in habit, but not in act. On the contrary, the precepts of the law concern the acts of the virtues;[2] but a habit does not come under a precept. Thus, this precept of the Apostle does not concern the habitual, but the actual resolution of our acts to God.

4. Moreover, the Lord fulfilled the precepts of the Old Law (*Matt.* v. 17), *I am not come to destroy, but to fulfill.* But this fulfillment is from the necessity of salvation, as is clear from what follows in this text (*Matt.* v. 20), *Unless your justice abound more than that of the Scribes and Pharisees, you shall not enter into the kingdom of heaven.* But everyone is bound to do those things which concern the necessity of salvation, and they are therefore bound to accomplish this fulfillment. But this aforesaid fulfillment pertains to perfection, for the Lord concluded (*Matt.* v. 48), *Be you therefore perfect, as also your heavenly Father is perfect.* Therefore all are bound to the perfection of charity.

5. Moreover, it is only the counsels that not all are bound to obey. But the perfection of eternal life or of charity is not referred to the counsels. For, a counsel of poverty is given, and it does not therefore follow that he who is poorer is more perfect; so, too, a counsel of virginity is given, and yet many virgins are less perfect in charity than others. Thus it seems that the perfection of charity is not referred to the counsels. Therefore no one is excused from the perfection of charity.[3]

6. Moreover, the status of bishops is more perfect than the status of religious. Otherwise, one would not be able lawfully to transfer from the state of a religious to that of a prelate. Thus, Dionysius says in the

---

[1] See *In III Sent.* d. 29, q. 1, a. 8, qa. 2.

[2] See *Sum. Theol.* I-II, q. 100, a. 2; q. 99, a. 2.

[3] See *Sum. Theol.* II-II, q. 184, a. 3; *Quodl.* IV, q. 12, a. 2, *ad.* 2m.

Eccles. Hierarchia,[4] that bishops are more perfect, but monks are more perfectly resigned in their virtues; and they ought to elevate themselves to that perfection which they observe in bishops. However, bishops are not bound to observe the counsel of poverty or other counsels of this kind. Therefore the perfection of charity does not consist in these.

7. Moreover, the Lord commanded many things to the Apostles which concern the perfection of this life, e.g., that they should not carry two coats or a pair of sandals or a staff or similar possessions. But what he enjoined on the Apostles, He enjoined on all, according to this *(Mark* xiii. 37), *What I say unto you, I say to all: watch.* Therefore all are bound to the perfection of life.

8. Moreover, whoever has charity loves eternal life more than temporal life. But each man is bound to the act of charity. Therefore each man is bound to choose eternal life over the life of the body. But, as Augustine says,[5] charity cries out when it has become perfect: *I desire to be dissolved and to be with Christ.* Therefore every one is bound to have perfect charity.

9. Moreover, Augustine says that perfect charity is such that one is even prepared to die for his brethren.[6] But all are bound to this, for it is written (I *John* iii. 16), *In this we have known the charity of God, because he hath laid down his life for us: and we ought to lay down our lives for the brethren.* Therefore every one is bound to the perfection of charity.

10. Moreover, every one is bound to avoid sin. But he who is without sin has some confidence on the day of judgment, for it is said (I *John* iv. 17), *In this is the charity of God perfected with us, that we may have confidence in the day of judgment.* Therefore all are bound to the perfection of charity.

11. Moreover, the Philosopher says in Book VIII of the *Ethic.,*[7] *we cannot give back equity to God and to parents; but it is sufficient that each one return to them what he is able.* But the perfection of charity consists in each one doing for God what he can, since no one can do more than that. Therefore each one is bound to have perfect charity.

12. Moreover, people in religion promise perfection of life. Therefore they seem to be bound to possess the perfection of charity and to have all those things which pertain to the perfection of life.

On the contrary, no one is bound to that which is not in him. But to

---

[4] Dionysius, *Ecclesiastica Hierarchia* VI; PG 3, 535, 538.
[5] See St. Augustine, *In Epist. Joan. ad Parthos* V, 3; PL 35, 2014.
[6] See St. Augustine, *De Doct. Christ.* I, 27; PL 34, 29.
[7] Aristotle, *Nic. Eth.* VIII, 7, 1158b 21.

have perfect charity is not from within us, but from God.[8] Therefore to possess perfect charity cannot be a precept.

I answer. It must be said that the answer to this problem can be seen from what has already been written.[9]

For, it was shown above,[10] that a certain kind of perfection is that which follows from the very species of charity, viz., that which consists in removing any inclination toward the contrary of charity. But another perfection, without which charity can exist, is that which pertains to the well-being of charity, viz., that which consists in the taking away of the occupations of the world by which human affection is hindered from freely advancing to God. But there is another kind of perfection of charity which is not possible for man in this life; and another which no created nature can attain. This is clear from what is written above.[11]

It is evident that all are said to be bound to that without which they cannot attain salvation. But without charity no one can attain eternal salvation, and when charity is possessed, eternal salvation is attained.

Thus all are bound to the first perfection of charity as to charity itself. To the second kind of perfection, without which charity can exist, men are not bound, since any sort of charity is sufficient for salvation. And even less are they bound to the third or fourth perfections, since no one is bound to the impossible.

To the first, it must be said that the wholeness of heart, considered as coming under the precept of charity, pertains to that perfection without which charity cannot exist.

To the second, it must be said that to order all things actually to God is not possible in this life; just as it is not possible to be always thinking of God, for this pertains to the perfection of heaven. But that all things be ordered to God by virtue does pertain to the perfection of charity, to which all are bound.

To prove this, it must be understood that just as in efficient causes the power of the primary cause remains in all the subsequent causes, so also does the intention of the principal end virtually remain in all the secondary ends. Thus, whoever actually intends some secondary end, virtually intends the primary end. For example, a physician, while actually gathering herbs, intends the end of preparing a prescription, while perhaps not thinking about health; virtually, however, he intends health as the end for which he administers the prescription.[12]

In the same way, he who orders himself to God as to an end, in all things which he does for his own sake, the intention of the final end which is God remains virtually. Thus he is able to gain merit in all things

---

[8] See Article X. [9] See Article V. [10] See Article V. [11] See Article X.
[12] See S.C.G. III, 18.

if he has charity.[13] It is in this manner, therefore, that the Apostle wrote that everything should be ordered to the glory of God.

To the third, it must be said that it is one thing to order things to God habitually and another thing to do so virtually. For, habitually one orders to God who does nothing, nor does he actually intend anything, as sleeping. But to order something to God virtually is the act of an agent ordering to God because of the end. Therefore to order to God habitually does not come under a precept, but to do so virtually does come from a precept since this is nothing other than to have God as the ultimate end.[14]

To the fourth, it must be said that the saying, *Be ye perfect, etc.*, seems to have reference to the love of enemies which in one way is from the perfection of a counsel; in another way from the necessity of a precept, as has been shown above.[15]

To the fifth, it must be said that the perfection of eternal life consists principally and essentially in certain things, but secondarily and accidentally it consists in others. Principally and essentially, this perfection consists in those things which pertain to an interior disposition of the mind, and especially in the act of charity which is the root of all the virtues.[16] But secondarily and accidentally, this perfection also consists in certain external things, such as virginity, poverty, and other such things.

These things are said to pertain to perfection in a threefold manner.

They pertain to perfection, first, insofar as through them the hindrances of the manifold activities of ordinary life are taken away from man, and when they are removed, the mind is more freely directed to God. Thus the Lord, when He said *(Matt.* xix. 21), *If thou wilt be perfect, go sell what thou hast, and give it to the poor,* He then added, *and come follow me.* He did this to show that poverty does not pertain to perfection unless it dispose one to follow Christ. For, we follow Him not with the movements of our body, but with the affections of the soul. In this way, the Apostle gave counsel about not marrying (I *Cor.* vii. 34), for *she who is a virgin thinkest on the things of the Lord, how to please Him.* And this same reasoning concerns similar cases.

Secondly, they pertain to perfection insofar as they are the effects of perfect charity; for he who loves God perfectly removes himself from those things which can prevent him from devoting himself to God.[17]

---

[13] See *Sum. Theol.* I-II, q. 114, a. 4; *De Virt. in Comm.* a. 2, *ad* 18m.
[14] See *Sum. Theol.* I-II, q. 100, aa. 9-10.
[15] See Article VIII.
[16] See *Sum. Theol.* II-II, q. 23, a. 8; *De veritate* q. 14, a. 5.
[17] See *Sum Theol.* II-II, q. 44, a. 1.

Thirdly, they pertain to the perfection of penance, for no satisfaction for sin can be equal to religious vows by which man consecrates himself to God; his soul through the vow of obedience, his body through the vow of chastity, and all other things through the vow of poverty.

Therefore, in regard to those things which primarily and essentially pertain to perfection, it follows that there will be a greater perfection where those things are found in more abundance; just as he who has more charity is more perfect. But with regard to those things which pertain to perfection as a consequent or accidentally, it does not follow that perfection in itself is greater where they are found in greater abundance. Therefore it does not follow that he who is poorer is more perfect. However, perfection in such matters ought to be measured by a comparison to those things in which perfection essentially consists. For example, he is said to be more perfect whose poverty separates him the more from earthly occupations and makes him freer in devoting himself to God.

To the sixth, it must be said that there is a difference between a friendship for a noble person and a friendship for a pleasant person, because in a friendship for a pleasant person, the friend is loved for the sake of pleasure; but in a friendship for a noble person, the friend is loved for his own sake, although pleasure is a result of this.[18] Therefore it is proper to the perfection of a friendship for a noble person that one who is occupied in serving a friend should sometimes even abstain from a pleasure which he experiences in the friend's presence for the sake of that friend. So, according to this friendship, he who would absent himself from a friend for the friend's sake would love him more than he who would not wish to depart from the presence of that friend even for that friend's sake. But if anyone be willingly and easily deprived of the friend's presence and be more pleased with other things, this proves that he loves the friend either not at all, or only a little.

We can, therefore, consider these three grades in charity, but God ought to be most especially loved for His own sake. For, there are some who freely, or without great vexation, are separated from the leisure of divine contemplation so that they are concerned with earthly affairs, and in these there is apparent either no charity, or very little. Some, however, so delight in the leisure of divine contemplation that they do not want to turn away from it even to apply their service to God to the salvation of their fellowmen. The highest degree, the third, are those who rise to the heights of charity so that even as they advance in divine contemplation, although they are very much delighted in it, serve God in order to save their fellowmen. This is the perfection meant by St. Paul (*Rom.* ix. 3). *For I wished myself to be an anathema from Christ*, i.e., separated

---

[18] See Aristotle, *Nic. Eth.* VIII, 3, 1156a 6.

[91]

from Him, *for my brethren;* and *(Philip.* i. 23-24), *I desire to be dissolved and to be with Christ,* . . . *But to abide still in the flesh, is needful for you.*

This is the perfection proper to prelates, preachers, and all the other religious whose life is dedicated to looking after the salvation of others. This is what is meant by the angels on the ladder, in Jacob's dream, ascending through contemplation, but descending through the responsibility which they bear over the salvation of their neighbor *(Gen.* xxviii. 11-12). The status of church dignitaries, however, cannot become less perfect because of some who misuse this state and seek that position for the sake of temporal goods, as if not attracted to the delightfulness of contemplation; just as the disbelief of many does not destroy faith in God, as is said *(Rom.* iii. 27).

To the seventh, it must be said that in the teaching of the Gospels, certain things are said to the Apostles in the person of all the faithful, viz., those things which pertain to the necessity of salvation. Thus, it is written *(Mark* xiii. 37), *What I say to you, I say to all: watch.* By *watch* is meant that solicitude which man ought to have so that he will not be found unprepared by Christ. But other things are said to the Apostles which concern the perfection of this life and the duties of prelates, and these cannot be included in, *What I say to you, I say to all.*

However, it should be understood that what the Lord said to His disciples *(Luke* ix. 3), *Take nothing for your journey, etc.,* as Augustine has explained in the *De Consen. Evangelist.,*[19] does not pertain to the perfection of life but to the power of apostolic dignity, through which the Apostles, while carrying nothing with them, were able to live on that which was provided for them by those to whom they preached the Gospel. Thus it was written in the same place *(Luke* x. 7), *The labourer is worthy of his hire,* i.e., of his food; but this was neither a precept nor a counsel, but a concession. Because of this, St. Paul who carried his necessities about with him, not using this concession, paid over and above, as if striving against his own wages. This is clear from I *Cor.* ix. 7.

To the eighth, it must be said that there are two affections in man; the one of charity by which the soul desires to be with Christ; the other, however, a natural affection by which the soul resists the separation from the body—which is natural to man; for not even was the *old man* taken away from Peter, as Augustine says in *Super Joan.*[20] Thus, by uniting these two affections, the soul wishes to be united in such a way to God so that it would not be separated from the body. For this reason, the Apostle wrote (II *Cor.* v. 4), *We would not be unclothed, but clothed*

[19] St. Augustine, *De Consensu Evangelistorum* II, 30; PL 34, 1112-1114.
[20] St. Augustine, *Tract. in Joan.* CXXIII; PL 35, 1969.

upon, that that which is mortal may be swallowed up by life. But since this is impossible, *While we are in the body, we are absent from the Lord* (II *Cor.* v. 6), opposition arises among these mentioned affections, and the more perfect charity is, the more does the affection of charity sensibly overcome the affection of nature. This pertains to the perfection of charity. Whence the Apostle adds (II *Cor.* v. 8), *But we are confident, and have a good will to be absent rather from the body, and to be present with the Lord.*

But in those in whom charity is imperfect, if only the affection of charity conquers, then from the repugnance of the natural affection, the victory of charity is rendered imperceptible. Therefore the Apostle clearly, unhesitatingly, and even boldly said, *I desire to be dissolved and to be with Christ (Philip.* i. 23); this is perfect charity. It is from the necessity of charity that the soul prefers in any way, even imperceptibly, the enjoyment of God to the union with the body.

To the ninth, it must be said that to give up your life, i.e., this present life for your brother is, in one way, from the necessity of charity, and in another way from the perfection of it.[21] For, man ought to love his neighbor more than his own body. Therefore, in the case where one is bound to look after the salvation of his neighbor, he is also bound to expose his bodily life to dangers for the sake of that salvation. But this is perfect charity, that he also expose his bodily life to dangers for those to whom he is not bound as to a neighbor.[22]

To the tenth, it must be said that, although every one is bound to live without mortal sin, it is not for every one to have complete assurance in this matter; but only for the perfect who have completely overcome sin.[23]

To the eleventh, it must be said that man is bound to return to parents, and even more to God, all that he can. But according to the common mode of human life, no one is bound from the necessity of a precept to give more than he is able.

To the twelfth, it must be said that no one promises perfect charity, but some promise a state of perfection which consists in those things which are ordered as means to the perfection of charity, such as poverty or fastings. They are not bound to all things of this kind, but only to those which they promise. Thus, the perfection of charity does not accrue to them by their vows, but it is as an end to which they attempt to arrive by means of what they vow.[24]

---

[21] See *Sum. Theol.* II-II, q. 44, a. 8.
[22] See *Sum. Theol.* II-II, q. 44, a. 8.
[23] See *De veritate* q. 10, a. 10.
[24] See *De veritate* q. 10, a. 10.

ARTICLE XII

Whether Charity, Once Possessed, Can Be Lost?[1]

It seems that charity, once possessed, cannot be lost.

1. It is said (I *John* iii. 9), *Whosoever is born of God, committeth not sin: for his seed abideth in him, and he can not sin, because he is born of God.* But only the sons of God have charity, for this distinguishes the children of God's kingdom from the children of perdition, as Augustine says in Book XV of the *De Trinit.*[2] Therefore he who has charity cannot lose it by sinning.

2. Moreover, every virtue that is lost by sinning withers away through sin, as Augustine says, *Charity is an invisible unction which will be the foundation wherever it is and which cannot wither away; it is nourished by the heat of the sun so that it does not dry up.*[3] Therefore charity cannot be lost through sin.

3. Moreover, Augustine says in Book VIII of the *De Trin.*[4] that if love is not true it ought not to be called love. But, as he also says in *Ad Julianum Comitem,*[5] charity which is able to be lost was never true. Thus it was not charity. Therefore he who has charity cannot lose it by sinning.

4. Morever, Prosper says in the *De Contemplatione,*[6] *Charity is a right will inseparably united to God, free from any defilement, not knowing corruption, not liable to the fault of change; for when it is possessed, one neither was able, nor will he be able to sin.* Therefore charity, once possessed, cannot be lost through sin.

5. Moreover, Gregory says in one of his Homilies,[7] that the love of God does great works, if it is present. But no one loses charity by doing great works. Therefore if charity is in us, it cannot be lost.

6. Moreover, man loves God more by charity than he loves himself by a natural love. But the love of self is never lost through sin; therefore neither is charity.

7. Moreover, free will does not incline toward sin unless it be through something that moves to sinning. But that which moves to every sin is self-love, which, as Augustine says in Book XIV of the *De Civit. Dei,*[8]

---

[1] See *Sum. Theol.* II-II, q. 24, a. 11; S.C.G. IV, 70; *Ad Rom.* VIII, 7; *Ad Cor.* XIII, 3.
[2] St. Augustine, *De Trinit.* XV, 18; PL 42, 1082.
[3] See St. Augustine, *In Epist. Joan. ad Parthos* III; PL 35, 2004.
[4] St. Augustine, *De Trinit.* VIII, 7; PL 42, 956.
[5] See Paul the Deacon, *De Salutaribus Documentis* VII; PL 99, 202.
[6] Prosper of Aquitain, *Expositio Psalmorum* CII; PL 51, 289.
[7] See St. Gregory the Great, *In Evang.* II. Hom. 30; PL 76, 1221.
[8] St. Augustine, *De Civ. Dei* XIV, 28; PL 41, 436.

caused the city of Babylon. But charity does not allow this, as Dionysius says, *Divine love causes rapture, not allowing men to be lovers of self.*[9] Likewise, the desire of money is the root of all evils, as St. Paul says (I *Tim.* vi. 10). But neither does charity allow this, as Augustine says in the LXXXIII *Quaestionum.*[10] Therefore he who has charity cannot lose it by sinning.

8. Moreover, whoever has charity is directed by the spirit of God, according to this, *If you are led by the spirit, you are not under the law (Galat.* v. 18). But the Holy Spirit, since He is of infinite power, cannot fail in His action. Therefore it seems that one having charity cannot sin.

9. Moreover, no one sins against a habit that is in operation, for the Philosopher says in Book VII of the *Ethic.,*[11] one does not sin against science in its actual state, but only against science in its habitual state. But charity is always in operation, for Gregory says in one of his Homilies,[12] the love of God is never idle. Therefore one cannot sin against charity so that it can in this way be lost by sin.

10. Moreover, if anyone loses charity, he loses it either while he is possessing it or while he is not possessing it. But while he has it, he does not lose it through sin, because sin would then exist along with charity. Nor does he lose it when he does not have it, because he cannot lose what he does not have. Therefore in no way can charity be lost.

11. Moreover, charity is a sort of accident in the soul.[13] But accidents can fail in four ways. The first way is through the corruption of the subject. But charity is not deficient in this way because the human soul, which is its subject, is incorruptible. An accident fails in the second way through a defect of cause, as light fails in the air through an absence of the sun. But charity cannot fail in this way because its cause, which is God, is unfailing. An accident fails in a third way by a deficiency of its object, as paternity ceases through the death of a child. But neither is charity deficient in this way, because its object is the eternal good, which is God. In the fourth way, an accident fails through the action of its contrary agent, as the cold quality of water fails through the action of heat. But charity does not fail in this way because it is stronger than sin which is the agent acting against it, according to this (*Cantic.* viii. 6), *Love is strong as death;* and *(Cant.* viii. 7), *Many waters cannot quench charity.* Therefore charity can in no way fail in one who possesses it.

12. Moreover, for rational nature, sin is in the class of evil. But evil does not act except in virtue of the good, as Dionysius says in chap. IV

[9] See Dionysius, *De Div. Nom.* IV; PG 3, 775.
[10] St. Augustine, *Lib.* 83 *Quaest.* q. 36; PL 40, 25.
[11] Aristotle, *Nic. Eth.* VII, 8, 1151a 16; V, 6, 1134a 17.
[12] See St. Gregory the Great, *In Evang.* II, Hom. 30; PL 76, 1221.
[13] See *Sum. Theol.* II-II, q. 23, a. 3, *obj.* 3 and *ad* 3m.

of the *De Divin. Nomin.*[14] But one good is not contrary to another, as is said in the *Praedicamentis;*[15] and thus one good cannot destroy another, because each thing is destroyed by its contrary. Therefore charity cannot be destroyed by sin.

13. Moreover, if charity is destroyed by sin, it is destroyed either by existing sin or by non-existing sin. But it cannot be destroyed by existing sin, for then mortal sin would be existing along with charity.[16] Again, it cannot be destroyed by non-existing sin, because non-being cannot act. Therefore charity cannot be lost by sin in any way.

14. Moreover, if charity is lost by sin, charity and sin exist in the soul either at the same moment or at different moments. They cannot exist at the same moment, because then they would exist together.[17] Nor can charity exist at one instant, and sin at another; because it would then be necessary that there be a medium time during which man has neither charity nor sin, which cannot happen. Therefore charity cannot be lost through sin.

15. Moreover, the Master says in Book III of the *Sentent.,* d. 31,[18] perfect charity cannot be lost through sin.

16. Moreover, just as the intellect is related to the knowledge of the truth, so is the will related to the love of the good. But the intellect, by knowing anything whatever, knows the first truth. Therefore by loving anything good, the will loves the greatest good. But he who loves never sins unless he turn himself by his love to a mutable good. Therefore in every sin man loves the highest good, the love of which is charity. Therefore charity can never be lost by sin.

17. Moreover, just as there is a universal and a proper agent in the genus of efficient cause, so also is there in the genus of final cause. But the proper agent always acts in virtue of the universal agent. Therefore the proper end always moves the will in virtue of the final end. But the final end is God. Thus the same argument as above follows.

18. Moreover, charity is a sign that someone is a true disciple of Christ, according to this *(John* xiii. 35), *By this shall all men know that you are my disciples, if you have love one for another.* But he is not a true disciple of Christ who is not always His disciple, as Augustine says.[19] In explaining this text *(John* vi. 67), *After this many of His disciples turned back,* Augustine says that they were not true disciples of Christ;[20]

[14] Dionysius, *De Div. Nom.* IV; PG 3, 786.
[15] Aristotle, *Categ.* XI, 14a 24.
[16] See *Sum. Theol.* II-II, q. 24, a. 12.
[17] See *Sum. Theol.* II-II, q. 24, a. 12.
[18] Peter Lombard, *Sent.* III, xxxi, 3; II, 693.
[19] See St. Augustine, *Tract. in Joan.* XXVII; PL 35, 1619.
[20] See St. Augustine, *Tract. in Joan.* XXVII; PL 35, 1619.

and the Lord said *(John* viii. 31), *If you abide in my word, you shall be my disciples indeed.* Therefore he who does not remain in charity never had charity.

19. Moreover, every motion follows the direction of that which rules it. But charity is the ruler of the heart of the one who has charity, for it seizes the entire heart for itself, as is commanded *(Deut.* vi. 5), *Love the Lord thy God with thy whole heart.* Therefore the movement of the one who has charity follows according to charity; thus charity cannot be lost through sin.

20. Moreover, differences diversifying genus and species cannot exist together as the same in number. But corruptible and incorruptible are of different genera, as is said in Book X of the *Metaph.*[21] Therefore, since the charity of this life and the charity of heaven are the same in number, it seems that just as the charity of heaven cannot be destroyed, neither can the charity of this life.

21. Moreover, if charity is destroyed, it is destroyed either in something or in nothing. But it is not destroyed in something, because this concerns only form which is educed from the potency of matter. It cannot be destroyed in nothing, because God Who alone is able to make nothing out of something, just as He alone is able to make something out of nothing, never destroys charity. Both are equally far apart. Therefore it seems that charity cannot be lost.

22. Moreover, that by which sin is taken away cannot be destroyed by sin. But sin is taken away by charity, according to this (I *Peter* iv. 8), *Charity covereth a multitude of sins.* Therefore charity cannot be lost through sin.

23. Moreover, commenting on this text *(Psalms* xxvi. 2), *While the wicked draw near against me to eat my flesh,* Augustine says in a marginal gloss, *If a gift be taken away, the giver is restrained.*[22] But God Who is the giver of charity cannot be restrained. Therefore charity cannot be taken away by sin.

24. Moreover, the soul, through charity, is united to God; just as a spouse, according to a kind of spiritual marriage. But a bodily marriage cannot be dissolved by any disagreement that overshadows the marriage. Therefore charity cannot be taken away by sin, in which the soul disagrees with those things which pertain to God.

On the contrary, (1) it is said *(Apoc.* ii. 4), *But I have somewhat against thee, because thou hast left thy first charity.*

(2) Moreover, Gregory says in a Homily,[23] *God comes into the hearts*

---

[21] Aristotle, *Metaph.* X (I), 10, 1059a 8.
[22] St. Augustine, *Enarrationes in Psalmos* XXVI, 2; PL 35, 201.
[23] See St. Gregory the Great, *In Evang.* II, Hom. 30; PL 76, 1221.

of some, but he does not dwell there; for they regard God out of remorse, but in time of temptation they return to committing sins, as if they lamented these sins very little. But God does not come into the hearts of the faithful except through charity. Therefore one is able to lose charity after it is possessed by pursuing sin.

(3) Moreover, it is said of David that the Lord was with him (I *Kings* xvi. 13). But shortly after, he sinned by committing adultery and murder. However, God is in man through charity. Therefore after charity is once possessed, one can lose it by sinning mortally.

(4) Moreover, charity is the life of the soul, according to this (I *John* iii. 14), *We know that we have passed from death to life, because we love the brethren.* But natural life can be lost through natural death. Therefore the life of charity can also be lost through the death of mortal sin.

I answer. It must be said that the Master wrote in Book I, dist. 17,[24] that the charity in us is the Holy Spirit. But his intention was not to say that the very act of our love is the Holy Spirit, but rather that the Holy Spirit moves our soul to love God and neighbor; just as He moves our soul to the acts of the other virtues. But to the act of the other virtues, He moves the soul through certain habits of infused virtues, whereas to the act of love for God and neighbor He moves the soul without any habitual medium. Therefore, Peter's opinion was indeed true insofar as he maintained that the soul is moved by the Holy Spirit to love God and neighbor. However, it was imperfect in this respect that he did not posit in us a certain created habit by which the human will is perfected to the act of this kind of love. For, it is necessary that a habit of this kind be found in the soul, as was said above in Article I of this Question.

There is, therefore, a four-fold consideration of charity that can be made.

First, charity is considered on the part of the Holy Spirit moving the soul to the love of God and neighbor.[25] In this regard, it is necessary to say that the movement of the Holy Spirit is always efficacious according to its own intention. For, the Holy Spirit operates in the soul, dividing to everyone according as he will, as is written (I *Cor.* xii. 11). Therefore those to whom the Holy Spirit freely wishes to give a persevering movement of divine love, in them sin cannot drive out charity.[26] This cannot be, I say, on the part of the moving power, although it is possible on the part of the indetermination of free choice.[27] For, these are the gifts of God by which those who are liberated are most certainly liber-

---

[24] Peter Lombard, *Sent.* I, xvii, 1; I, 106.
[25] See *Sum. Theol.* II-II, q. 24, aa. 2-3.
[26] See *Sum. Theol.* II-II, q. 24, a. 10.
[27] See *Sum. Theol.* II-II, q. 24, a. 11.

ated, as Augustine says in *De Praedest. Sanctor.*[28] For though the Holy Spirit freely gives to some that at times they might be moved to love God, He does not give in such manner that they might persevere to the end in that love, as is clear from St. Augustine in *De Correct. et Gratia.*[29]

Secondly, charity is considered according to the power of that charity. In this respect, no one who possesses charity can sin, in the sense of committing a sin by virtue of that charity; just as no one possessing any form can act contrary to that form by virtue of the form. For example, that which is warm, although it can lose heat and become cold, cannot become cold or be cold by virtue of its warmth.[30] It was in this way that Augustine spoke in *De Sermone Domini in Monte,*[31] explaining this text *(Matt.* vii. 18), *A good tree cannot bring forth evil fruit.* For, he said that it can happen that what was snow is not now snow, but it does not happen that *snow* is *warm.* Thus, he who was evil is not now evil, but it cannot be that an evil man acts rightly. And concerning the good, this same reasoning applies to all the virtues, for no one uses virtue for evil.

Thirdly, there is a consideration of charity from the side of the will insofar as the will is subjected to charity, as matter is to form.[32] It must be noted that when form completes the entire potentiality of matter, the potency cannot remain in matter as potency to another form. Whence, it possesses that form in a manner such that it cannot be lost, as is evident with celestial matter.[33] But there is a certain form which does not complete the entire potentiality of matter, but it remains in potency to another form. Then that form is possessed in such a manner that it can be lost on the part of matter, i.e., on the subject; as is evident with the forms of the bodily elements. But charity completes the potentiality of its subject according as it reduces its subject to the act of love. Therefore in heaven, where the rational creature loves God in act with his whole heart, and loves nothing else except by referring it perfectly to God, charity is possessed in such a way that it is not lost. But in this present state of life, charity does not perfect all of the potentialities of the soul, and is not always perfectly directed to God because it must refer everything to Him by an actual intention. Therefore the charity of this life can be lost, considered on the part of the subject.[34]

The fourth consideration of charity is on the part of the subject according as it is compared in a special way to charity itself, as potency

---

[28] St. Augustine, *De Praedestinatione Sanctorum* VIII; PL 44, 972-973.
[29] St. Augustine, *De Correptione et Gratia* VIII; PL 44, 925-926.
[30] See *Sum. Theol.* II-II, q. 24, a. 12.
[31] St. Augustine, *De Serm. Domini in Monte* II, 24; PL 34, 1305-1306.
[32] See *Sum. Theol.* II-II, q. 24, a. 1.
[33] See *Sum. Theol.* II-II, q. 24, a. 11.
[34] See *Sum. Theol.* II-II, q. 24, aa. 8, 11.

is compared to habit. It must be considered that the habit of virtue inclines man to act rightly according as through it man has the right estimation of the end. For, as is said in Book III of the *Ethic.*,[35] according as a man is, such does the end seem to him. For example, just as taste judges flavor insofar as it is the affection for some good or bad disposition, so also that which is suitable to man according to a habitual disposition, inhering in him either as good or evil, is judged by him as a good; and what is not in accord with this is considered as evil and repugnant. Whence the Apostle says (I *Cor.* ii. 14), *The sensual man perceiveth not these things that are of the spirit of God.*

But it sometimes happens that that which seems to one to be according to the inclination of habit does not seem to him to be according to something else. For example, to one who has carnal delight, the delight of the flesh seems to be a good according to the inclination of his proper habit; but it seems to be contrary to the good according to the deliberation of reason or the text of Scripture. And because of this estimation, one who has the habit of carnal delight sometimes acts contrary to that habit. Likewise, one who has the habit of virtue sometimes acts contrary to the inclination of his proper habit; for a thing seems to him to be otherwise, according to some other mode, such as through passion or anything that entices him from the correct estimation.[36]

Therefore, no one will be able to act contrary to the habit of charity, because no one is able to have any judgment about the end and the object of charity other than that which he has according to the inclination of charity. This, however, will be in heaven where the very essence of God, which is the essence of goodness, will be seen. Thus, just as now no one can wish anything unless it be under the aspect of good, nor is any one able not to love the good as good; so also in the next life, no one will be able not to love this good, which is God. Because of this, no one who sees God in His essence can act against charity; and that is why the charity of heaven cannot be lost.[37]

However, now our mind does not see that essence of divine goodness; it sees some of its effects which can seem either good or not-good, according to different considerations. For, the spiritual good appears as not-good to some insofar as it is contrary to their carnal delight, which concupiscence desires.[38] Therefore the charity of this life can be lost through mortal sin.[39]

---

[35] Aristotle, *Nic. Eth.* III, 5, 1114a 32.
[36] See *Sum. Theol.* I-II, q. 51, a. 3; q. 53, a. 1; *De Virt. in Comm.* aa. 1, 9.
[37] See *Sum. Theol.* II-II, q. 26, a. 13.
[38] See *Sum. Theol.* II-II, q. 24, a. 8; q. 27, a. 4.
[39] See *Sum. Theol.* II-II, q. 24, aa. 10-12.

To the first, it must be said that what St. John wrote (I *John* iii. 9), should be understood according to the power of the Holy Spirit moving the soul, Who unfailingly operates as He wishes.

To the second, it must be said that Augustine speaks of charity as the power of charity itself;[40] for charity is sufficient that it will never wither away. But that it is lost, is due to the indetermination of the subject, as has been said.[41]

To the third, it must be said that true love has an essential note that is never lost; for he who truly loves man has foremost in his soul that he will never diminish that love. But when this commitment in the soul is changed, that which was true love is lost. Further, if anyone would have this commitment that he would sometimes cease loving, his love would not be true. Whence it is clear that charity, considered according to its own power cannot be lost; but it can be lost because of the indeterminate power of the subject.

To the fourth, it must be said that Prosper also speaks of charity according to the power of charity itself, and not according to the power of the subject.[42]

To the fifth, it must be said that charity, if it is present, has an inclination to do great works, and Gregory wished to speak in this manner according to the quality of his own virtue.[43] But sometimes one can fail from this because of the indetermination of the subject.

To the sixth, it must be said that since there is in man a twofold nature, viz., the intellectual which is primary, and the sensitive which is lesser; he truly loves himself who loves himself for the good of reason. But when a man loves himself and wants sensual goods for himself which are contrary to the good of reason, he hates himself more than he loves himself, because it is written (*Psalms* x. 6), *He that loveth iniquity hateth his own soul.* And this the Philosopher also said in Book IX of the *Ethic*.[44] According to this, true love of self is lost through the contrary sin; just as the love of God is also lost.

To the seventh, it must be said that charity excludes every movement of sin according to its own determination. For, it pertains to the essence of charity that it wishes not to desire concupiscibly, nor to love self inordinately. But sometimes the contrary happens because of the indetermination of free choice and the corruption of nature; thus the Apostle said *(Rom.* vii. 19), *For the good which I will, I do not; but the evil which I will not, that I do.*

[40] See St. Augustine, *In Epist. Joan. ad Parthos* III; PL 35, 2004.
[41] See the Reply to this Article.
[42] See Prosper of Aquitain, *In Psalm.* CII; PL 51, 289.
[43] See St. Gregory the Great, *In Evan.* II, Hom. 30; PL 76, 1221.
[44] Aristotle, *Nic. Eth.* IX, 4, 1166b 15.

To the eighth, it must be said that whenever one follows the move-ment of the Holy Spirit, he does not sin; but when he resists it, then he sins.

To the ninth, it must be said that the being *(esse)* of charity is not always to be in operation, otherwise when one sleeps, he would not have charity. But it is said that the love of God is never idle according to the determination of charity, whose whole purpose is that a man give him-self completely to God.[45]

To the tenth, it must be said that a loss is related to the thing had, as corruption is related to the thing existing. Therefore, as corruption begins in an existing thing and terminates in its non-being *(non-esse)*, because the change is from being *(esse)* to non-being *(non-esse);* so does a loss, since it is a change from having to non-having, begin in having and terminate in non-having.[46] Therefore the beginning of the loss of charity is when charity is had; its end, however, is when charity is not had.

To the eleventh, it must be said that charity ceases to exist in the soul in some way according to these four modes. For, the subject of charity, although it is incorruptible according to its substance, becomes indisposed to this form through the contrary disposition of sin. Likewise, although the cause of charity is incorruptible, the influence of this cause is impeded by sin which separates us from God. Also, charity fails on the part of its object insofar as the will diverts itself from the unchange-able good. Charity even fails through the contrary movement to sinning; for, essentially speaking, although sin is weaker than charity, in some instances sin can be stronger, viz., when charity is not operating in act and the movement of sin directs toward some other particular opera-tion. The Philosopher also showed in Book VII of the *Ethic.,*[47] that science, although it is stronger, can be overcome by passion; this is con-sidered insofar as the agent is not in act but is bound up in habit be-cause of passion. For, just as science is strongest in the universal, passion however operates in the particular;[48] so also charity is strongest when acting toward the final end, but it allows the movement of sin which has strength in some particular act.

To the twelfth, it must be said that the Philosopher did write that the good of one virtue is not contrary to the good of another, and this is what he intended to say in the *Praedicamentis* and in Book II of the

[45] See St. Gregory the Great, *In Evang.* II, Hom. 30; PL 76, 1221.
[46] See Aristotle, *On Generation and Corruption* I, 4, 319b 32-320a 2; *Phys.* V, 1, 225a 1-20; *Metaph.* X (I), 10, 1058b 36-1059a 9.
[47] Aristotle, *Nic. Eth.* VII, 3, 1147a 10.
[48] See Aristotle, *Nic. Eth.* VII, 3, 1147a 32.

Ethic.[49] But in nature, one good is contrary to another, for each of the contraries is a certain good of nature. Therefore, the good which moves the appetite to sin is contrary to the divine good which is the object of charity, insofar as the end is found in the divine good. For there can be only one final end; just as in a kingdom, where there can be only one king, he who makes himself to be a king is contrary to the actual king, according to what is written *(John* xix. 12), *Whosoever maketh himself a king, speaketh against Caesar.*

To the thirteenth, it must be said that charity is not driven out by sin as by an agent, but as by its contrary. Thus, that intervening of sin is the expulsion of charity; just as the coming of light is the expulsion of darkness. For, the light drives out darkness by its own becoming; but a movement to sin drives out charity according as it pre-exists in the understanding of the soul.

To the fourteenth, it must be said that when man stands in mortal sin, this is done by a certain deliberation of reason; for without a deliberating consent, there can be no mortal sin. But this deliberation is a measured movement of time in the last moment of which sin exists in the soul. But before that final instant, the nearest instant in which charity exists cannot be designated; because these moments are not regarded as moments following one another, for time is a continuum. Therefore in the entire time which precedes the moment that terminates in the final instant, charity exists in the soul; after the last instant of this time, sin exists. Thus it is not possible to designate the final instant in which charity exists, but the final time, as is shown by the Philosopher in Book VIII of the *Physic.*[50]

To the fifteenth, it must be said that if the Master understood of charity that it is the charity of heaven,[51] it is true that it is not lost, according to the proofs given above. But if he meant the charity of this life insofar as it is perfect, it is not true that it cannot be lost because of the mode of inhering in its subject, but only by virtue of the movement of the Holy Spirit; and thus it is said that those who were strengthened, were strengthened in this life.

To the sixteenth, it must be said that just as the first truth is understood in the knowledge of anything that is true, as the first exemplar is understood in an image or vestige, so is the highest good loved in the love of anything that is good. But such a love of the highest good is not sufficient for the definition of charity; it is necessary that the highest good be loved as the object of beatitude.

[49] Aristotle, *Categ.* X, 12a 15; *On Interpretations* XIV, 23b 7; *Nic. Eth.* II, 6, 1106a 15.
[50] Aristotle, *Phys.* VIII, 1, 251b 25; IV, 11, 220a 25.
[51] See Peter Lombard, *Sent.* III, xxxi, 3; II, 693.

[103]

The answer to the seventeenth objection is evident from this.

To the eighteenth, it must be said that, as Augustine says explaining this text *(John x. 27)*, *My sheep hear my voice and do not hear the voice of others,* there is a certain voice of Christ which no one hears unless he be His sheep through a predetermination. This voice says, *He who perseveres to the end will be saved.* And in this way he understands that he who does not remain faithful to the words of Christ is not a true disciple, because he has not learned from Him to persevere effectively.[52] However, he can be a temporary disciple when he loves God for a time and his neighbor.

To the nineteenth, it must be said that as long as charity is actually dominant in man, man is not moved by a contrary motion, but he follows the movement of charity. Therefore the greatest remedy against sin is for man to return into his heart, converting it to the love of God. But when man is not moved in act according to charity, he is under pressure from the contrary movement of sin.

To the twentieth, it must be said that to be corrupted and to be generated or to become, is proper to that which has being *(esse)*; i.e., only a thing subsisting in its being *(esse)*. But accidents and forms that are not subsisting are not called being because they have existence, but rather because by them something exists. Therefore, to become and to be corrupted are not proper to accidents and to forms, but to subjects.[53] For example, when any thing becomes white, this is whiteness in becoming; just as for any thing to be white, is this existing whiteness. And the same reasoning holds for corruption. Therefore corruptible and incorruptible are not attributed directly to accidents, but only to substance. Whence, there is nothing that prevents the charity of this life and of heaven from being the same in number; although the charity here can be lost while the charity of heaven cannot be lost.[54]

To the twenty-first, it must be said that, as has already been said,[55] charity, properly speaking, is not corrupted; but the subject ceases to participate in charity. Whence it is not proper to say that charity is corrupted either in something or in nothing.

To the twenty-second, it must be said that because of the indetermination of the subject, just as charity that overshadows sin destroys it, so also does sin overshadowing charity, drives it out; for contraries are mutually exclusive.

---

[52] See St. Augustine, *Tract. in Joan.* XLVIII; PL 35, 1742.
[53] See Aristotle, *De Gen. et Corrup.* I, 4, 319b 32-320a 2; *Phys.* V, 1, 225a 1-20; *Metaph.* X (I), 10, 1058b 36-1059a 9.
[54] See *Sum. Theol.* II-II, q. 26, a. 13.
[55] See the Reply to this Article.

To the twenty-third, it must be said that if a gift can be taken away by violence, then it seems that the giver who must preserve the gift for the one to whom he has bestowed it, is defeated.[56] But if he to whom the gift is given voluntarily rejects it, it does not seem that this causes the donor, who ought not to force men to virtue, to be defeated.

To the twenty-fourth, it must be said that a wife in marriage loses the power over her own body. But the soul, through charity, does not lose the power of free choice. Whence the argument does not follow.

[56] See St. Augustine, *In Psalm* XXVI, 2; PL 35, 201.

ARTICLE XIII

Whether Charity Can Be Lost Through One Act of Mortal Sin?[1]

It seems that charity cannot be lost through one act of mortal sin.

1. For, Origen writes in I *Periarch.*,[2] *If a disgust for spiritual things ever takes one who has continually stayed in the highest and perfect state, I do not think that he is taken away or falls away suddenly; but he must fall away little by little and gradually. Thus, as it can sometimes happen, if one undergoes a slight fall and quickly recovers, it does not seem that he rushes to his complete downfall.* But he who hast lost charity falls completely, according to this (I *Cor.* xiii. 2), *If I have not charity, I am nothing.* Therefore charity is not lost through one mortal sin which sometimes happens suddenly.

2. Moreover, Bernard says in the *De Diligendo Deo*,[3] charity was not extinct in Peter who denied Christ, but it was only rendered inactive. But when he denied Christ, he sinned mortally. Therefore charity is not lost through one act of mortal sin.

3. Moreover, Pope Leo the Great says in Sermon IX *De Passione*,[4] when speaking of Peter, *Our Lord saw in you not a conquered faith, not a reverted love, but a constancy shaken. Tears flowed in abundance where affection never failed, and the fount of charity washed away the words of dread.* Therefore the love of charity was not lacking in Peter on account of that act of mortal sin.

4. Moreover, charity is stronger than acquired virtue. But acquired virtue is not corrupted by one act of sin; just as it is not generated by one act, for the Philosopher says in Book II of the *Ethic.*,[5] virtue is generated and corrupted from the same thing. Therefore much less is charity lost through the act of one mortal sin.

5. Moreover, a thing is not driven out except by its contrary. But the habit of charity is not opposed to the act of sin. Now habit is not generated by one act.[6] Therefore charity is not lost by one act of sin.

6. Moreover, just as faith is concerned with believing many things, so is charity concerned with loving many things out of charity. But he who does not believe in one article of faith does not on that account lose faith in the other articles.[7] Therefore he who sins against one object

---

[1] See *Sum. Theol.* II-II, q. 24, a. 12; *In III Sent.* d. 31, q. 1, a. 1.
[2] Origen, *Peri Archon* I, 3; PG 11, 155.
[3] See William of St. Thierry, *De Nat. et Dign. Amoris* c. VI; PL 184, 390.
[4] Pope Leo the Great, *Sermones* LX; PL 54, 345.
[5] Aristotle, *Nic. Eth.* II, 1, 1103b 7; II, 2, 1104a 26.
[6] See *Sum. Theol.* I-II, q. 51, a. 3.
[7] See *Sum. Theol.* II-II, q. 1, a. 7; q. 2, a. 6; q. 4, aa. 3-4; *De veritate* q. 14, aa. 5, 7.

that should be loved out of charity does not on this account lose charity toward the other objects of love. Thus charity is not lost by one mortal sin.

On the contrary, it is written (I John iii. 17), *He that hath the substance of this world, and shall see his brother in need, and shall shut up his bowels from him: how doth the charity of God abide in him?* Thus it seems that through a sin of omission one can lose charity. But a sin of transgression is no less than a sin of omission. Therefore charity is taken away by any sin.

I answer. It must be said that, without doubt, the habit of charity is taken away by one act of mortal sin, for a sin is not called mortal unless men die spiritually by it; which cannot happen with charity which is the life of the soul. Likewise, man also becomes worthy of eternal death through mortal sin, according to this *(Rom.* vi. 23), *The wages of sin is death.* But whoever has charity is worthy of eternal life, for the Lord promised to those who love Him a manifestation of His own self in which vision eternal life consists. Whence it must be said that man loses charity through any act of mortal sin. For, it is clear that in each act of mortal sin there is a turning away from the immutable good to which charity unites us. The act of mortal sin is opposed to this charity.[8]

Now, because act is not directly contrary to habit but to act, one could see that through the act of mortal sin the opposite act of charity would be hindered; however, not so that the habit would be taken away, as it happens in acquired habits. For, no one loses the virtue of generosity if he acts contrary to that virtue.[9]

This is not the case concerning the habit of charity. For, the habit of charity does not have a cause in the subject, but entirely depends on an extrinsic cause; for the charity of God is poured forth in our hearts, by the Holy Spirit, Who is given to us, as is written *(Rom.* v. 5). However, God does not cause charity in our soul so that He is the cause only of its becoming and not of its preservation; as the builder is the cause of a house only in its becoming, and when he is taken away, the house still remains. God, however, is the cause of charity and of grace in the soul both as regards their becoming and their preservation; just as the sun is the cause of light in the air. Therefore, just as light in the air immediately ceases if some obstacle is placed in the way, so does the habit of charity immediately cease in the soul when the soul turns itself away from God through sin.[10] This is what Augustine says in Book VIII of *Super Gen. ad Litteram,*[11] *God does not operate in a just man thus* (that

⁸ See *Sum. Theol.* II-II, q. 24, a. 12.
⁹ See *Sum. Theol.* II-II, q. 24, a. 12.
¹⁰ See *Sum. Theol.* II-II, q. 24, a. 120.
¹¹ St. Augustine, *De Genesi ad Litteram* VIII, 12; PL 34, 383.

is, by justifying him), *so that if He would depart, that which He effected would remain in His absence. Rather, just as the air has not made itself lucid but becomes so in the presence of light, so man is illuminated when God is present to him; but he continues in darkness when God is absent.*

To the first, it must be said that this saying of Origen can be understood in this way, that a man who is in a perfect state does not suddenly fall into the act of mortal sin, but does so through some previous negligence. But because he adds, *If one undergoes a slight fall,* etc., it seems better to say that he understood: one who completely falls away falls so that he sins by malice, which fall does not come about suddenly.[12] For, as the Philosopher says in Book I of the *Ethic.,*[13] it is not easy for a just man to perform unjust works suddenly as an unjust man does them, viz., by choice. Therefore one loses charity through one act of mortal sin, but some of the previous perfection remains if he has not lost charity out of malice.

To the second, it must be said that charity is lost in two ways; directly and indirectly. It is lost directly through an actual contempt for God, as happens with those who say to God *(Job* xxi. 14), *Depart from us, we desire not the knowledge of thy ways.* In another way, it is lost indirectly; just as one who is not thinking of God, consents to something that is against the law of God on account of some passion of fear or of concupiscence, and as a consequence loses charity.

Therefore Bernard intended to say that charity was not extinct in Peter according to the first manner; but Peter lost it according to the second manner, and therefore Bernard calls it inactive.[14] In the same way, the words of Leo should be understood, and this is clear from what he further adds, *The cleansing remedy will not be far away where there was no judgment of the will;*[15] for the denial of Peter was driven by fear more than by a deliberate judgment of the will.

From this the answer to the third objection is clear.

To the fourth, it must be said that an acquired virtue has its cause in the subject and is not entirely extrinsic, as is true of charity. Therefore the comparison between acquired virtue and charity cannot be made.

To the fifth, it must be said that in contraries, one contrary can be driven out without the other contrary coming in. But the habits of virtue and vice are mediated contraries; whence the Philosopher says in the *Praedicamentis,*[16] there is a medium between good and evil. Whence it

[12] See Origen, *Peri Archon* I, 3; PG 11, 155.
[13] Aristotle, *Nic. Eth.* II, 4, 1105a 31.
[14] See William of St. Thierry, *De Nat. et Dign. Amoris* c. VI; PL 184, 390.
[15] See Pope Leo the Great, *Serm.* LX; PL 54, 345.
[16] Aristotle, *Categ.* X, 12a 15; *Periherm.* XIV, 23b 7.

is not necessary to say that a man loses the habit of one virtue only when the habit of the contrary vice is generated in him.

To the sixth, it must be said that a habit, of itself, regards the formal notion of its object more than the material notion of the object; therefore if the formal notion *(ratio)* of the object is taken away, the species of habit does not remain.

However, the formal notion in the object of faith is the first truth manifested through the teaching of the Church; just as the formal notion of science is the medium of demonstration.[17] Therefore, just as one who remembers the conclusions of geometry does not have the science of geometry if he does not assent to these conclusions because of the reasons of geometry, but he holds these conclusions only as opinion; so also one who holds those things which are of faith but does not assent to them because of the authority of Catholic teaching, does not have the habit of faith. For, he who asserts to anything because of Catholic teaching assents to all those things which that teaching contains. Otherwise, he would believe himself more than the teaching of the Church. From this it is clear that he who obstinately denies one article of faith does not have faith in the other articles—that faith, I say, which is an infused habit,[18]—for he holds the conclusions of faith as opinion.

---

[17] See *Sum Theol.* II-II, q. 1, aa. 1, 5; *De veritate*, q. 14, a. 8.
[18] See *Sum. Theol.* II-II, q. 6, a. 1; *De veritate* q. 14, aa. 2-3; *De Virt. in Comm.* a. 10.

LIST OF BOOKS USED

Ambrosiaster. *In Epistolam B. Pauli ad Corinthios,* Migne PL, vol. 17.
————. *In Epistolam ad Romanos,* Migne PL, vol. 17.

The Apocryphal New Testament. Translated by M. R. James. Oxford: Clarendon Press, 1955.

Aristotle, *Aristotelis Opera,* ed. Academia Regia Borussica, ex recognitione I. Bekker. 2 vols. Berlin: G. Reimer, 1831.
————. *The Works of Aristotle.* Translated by W. D. Ross and others. 11 vols. Oxford: Clarendon Press, 1928-31.
————. *The Basic Works of Aristotle,* ed. R. McKeon. New York: Random House, 1941.

Augustine, St. *Confessionum,* Migne PL, vol. 32.
————. *De Duabus Animabus,* Migne PL, vol. 32.
————. *De Moribus Ecclesiae,* Migne PL, vol. 32.
————. *De Libero Arbitrio,* Migne PL, vol. 32.
————. *Epistolae,* Migne PL, vol. 33.
————. *De Vera Religione,* Migne PL. vol. 34.
————. *De Sermone Domini in Monte,* Migne PL, vol. 34.
————. *De Genesi ad Litteram,* Migne PL, vol. 34.
————. *De Doctrina Christiana,* Migne PL, vol. 34.
————. *De Consensu Evangelistarum,* Migne PL, vol. 34.
————. *In Joanis Evangelium,* Minge PL, vol. 35.
————. *Enarrationes in Psalmos,* Migne PL, vol. 36.
————. *In Epistolam Joannis ad Parthos,* Migne PL, vol. 35.
————. *Sermones,* Migne PL, vol. 38.
————. *Enchiridion,* Migne PL, vol. 40.
————. *De Diversis Quaestionibus* LXXXIII, Migne PL, vol. 40.
————. *De Civitate Dei,* Migne PL, vol. 41.
————. *De Natura Boni,* Migne PL, vol. 42.
————. *De Trinitate,* Migne PL, vol. 42.
————. *Contra Faustum,* Migne PL, vol. 42.
————. *Contra Julianum,* Migne PL, vol. 44.
————. *De Praedestinatione Sanctorum,* Migne PL, vol. 44.
————. *De Correptione et Gratia,* Migne PL, vol. 44.

Bernard, St. *De Diligendo Deo,* Migne PL, vol. 182.
————. *Sermones in Cantica Canticorum,* Migne PL, vol. 183.
————. *Sermones de Tempore,* Migne PL, vol. 183.

Bourke, V. J. "Introduction to St. Thomas on Truth," in *Truth,* Chicago: Henry Regnery Co., 1952.

Chenu, M. D. *Introduction a l'étude de saint Thomas d'Aquin.* Montréal: Institut l'Étude Médiévaux, 1950.
————. *Le théologie comme science au XIII$_e$ siècle* (2 éd.). Paris: Vrin, 1943.
————. "Un essai de méthode théologique aux XII$_e$ siècle," *Revue des Sciences Philosophique et Théologique,* Paris: Vrin, 1935.

Destrez, J. *Études critiques sur les oeuvres de s. Thomas d'Aquin, Bibliotheque Thomiste,* Vol. XVII. Paris: 1933.

Dionysius. *De Divinis Nominibus,* Migne PG, vol. 3.
————. *Ecclesiastica Hierarchia,* Migne PG, vol. 3.

[110]

Eschmann, I. T. "A Catalogue of St. Thomas' Works," in *The Christian Philosophy of St. Thomas Aquinas.* New York: Random House, 1956.

Fitzpatrick, M. and Wellmuth, J. *On Spiritual Creatures,* Milwaukee: Marquette University Press, 1949.

Glorieux, P. "Les Questions Disputées de S. Thomas et leur suite chronologie," in *Recherches de théologie ancienne et medievale,* 1932.

Grabmann, M. *Die Werke des heilige Thomas von Aquin,* Beiträge Münster, XXII, 1931.
_____. *Die echten Schriften des heilige Thomas von Aquin.* Münster, 1949.

Gregory the Great, St. *Moralium,* Migne PL, vol. 75.
_____. *Homilarium in Evangelia,* Migne PL, vol. 76.
_____. *Epistolarum,* Migne PL, vol. 77.
_____. *Regulae Pastoralis,* Migne PL, vol. 77.
_____. *Super Ezechiel,* PL, vol. 76.

Jerome, St. *In Evangelium Matthaei,* Migne PL, vol. 26.

Keeler, L. W. *Sancti Thomae Aquinatis, Tractatus de Spiritualibus Creaturis.* Rome: Gregoriana, 1938.

Koch, J. *Ueber die Reihenfolge der Questiones Disputatae des hl. Thomas von Aquin, Philosophische Jahrbuch,* 1924, XXXVII.

LaGrange, M. J. *The Gospel of Jesus Christ,* translated by the English Dominicans. 2 vols. in 1. London: Burns, Oates and Washbourne, 1950.

Leo the Great, Pope. *Sermones,* Migne PL, vol. 54.

Lombard, Peter. *Petri Lombardi Libri IV Sententiarum,* ad Claras Aquas ex Typographis Collegii S. Bonaventurae, 1916, 2 vols.

Lottin, O. "Les dons du Saint-Esprit chez les théologiens depuis P. Lombard jusqu'à S. Thomas d'Aquin," *Recherches de théologie ancienne et medievale,* 1929, pp. 41-97.

Madonnet, P. *Des écrits authentiques de s. Thomas* (2 ed.). Fribourg: 1910.
_____. "Chronologie des Questions Disputées de Saint Thomas d'Aquin," *Revue Thomiste,* 1918.

Origen, *Peri Archon;* Migne PG, vol. 11.
_____. *In Canticum Canticorum,* Migne PG, vol. 13.

Paré, G., Brunet, A., and Tremblay, P. *La Renaissance du XII$_e$ siècle. Les écoles et l'enseignement,* Institut d'Études Médievale d'Ottawa, 1933, III.

Paul the Deacon. *De Salutaribus Documentis,* Migne PL, vol. 99.

Pession, P. M. "Introductio Generalis," *Quaestiones disputatae saint Thomae,* vol. I, Turin: 1949.

Prosper of Aquitain. *Expositio Psalmorum,* Migne PL, vol. 51.

Reid, J. P. *On the Virtues (in General).* Providence: College Press, 1951.

Synave, P. "Le catalogue officiel des oeuvres de saint Thomas d'Aquin," *Archives,* vol. III. 1928.
_____. "Le problème chronologique des Questions Disputées de saint Thomas d'Aquin," *Revue Thomiste,* 1926.

[111]

Thomas Aquinas, St. *St. Thomae Aquinatis Doctoris Angelici Opera Omnia,* iussu impensaque Leonis XIII P.M. edita, ex Romae Typographia Polyglotta, 1882-1948, 16 vols.

_____. *Opera Omnia,* ed. E. Fretté and P. Maré. 34 vols. Paris: Vivès, 1872-1880. 34 vols.
_____. *Summa Theologiae,* 5 vols. Ottawa: 1941-1945.
_____. *Basic Writings of St. Thomas Aquinas,* ed. A. C. Pegis. 2 vols. New York: Random House, 1945.
_____. *Summa Contra Gentiles,* Leonine: Rome, 1934.
_____. *On the Truth of the Catholic Faith.* 4 vols. New York: Doubleday and Co., Inc., 1955-56.
_____. *Scriptum super Libros Sententiarum Magistri Petri Lombardi,* ed. R. P. Mandonnet. 3 vols. Paris: 1929-1933.
_____. *Quaestiones Disputatae.* 2 vols. Turin: 1949.
_____. *Truth.* 3 vols. Chicago: Henry Regnery Co., 1952-1954.
_____. *Quaestiones Quodlibetales.* Turin: 1927.

Van Steenberghen, F. *Siger dans l'histoire d'Aristotelisme.* Louvain: 1942.

Walz, A. "Saint Thomas d'Aquinas Écrits," in *Dictionnaire de théologie catholique,* 1946. XV, 1.

William of St. Thierry, *De Natura et Dignitate Amoris,* Migne PL, vol. 184.

INDEX

Accident: is being in another, 95, 104; and charity, 95

Act: of charity, 41; perfection of, 47

Actions: genus and nature of, 24; of intellect, 38; of will, 38

Affection: of charity, 92-93; and love, 28; of will, 92-93

Agent: imperfect, 24; instrumental, 21; moves to action, 22; proper, 96

Ambrosiaster, 35, 110

Apocryphal New Testament, 68, 73, 110

Appetite, natural, 76

Aristotle, 18, 23, 25, 26, 27, 28, 29, 30, 31, 33, 35, 36, 39, 40, 41, 42, 43, 46, 47, 48, 51, 52, 53, 55, 56, 58, 59, 60, 61, 64, 67, 68, 70, 71, 72, 77, 78, 88, 91, 95, 96, 97, 100, 101, 102, 103, 104, 106, 108, 110

Augustine, St., 13, 17, 18, 19, 20, 23, 24, 26, 27, 28, 30, 35, 36, 37, 40, 41, 43, 46, 47, 51, 54, 58, 60, 61, 66, 67, 69, 70, 71, 74, 76, 78, 81, 82, 84, 86, 88, 92, 94, 95, 96, 97, 99, 101, 104, 105, 107, 110

Bernard, St., 20, 27, 74, 110

Body: burden of, 83; love of, 59, 60, 62, 64, 77

Bourke, V. J., 3, 110

Brunet, A., 3, 111

Cause: efficient, 89, 96; final, 96; and number, 35; and genus, 40

Charity: active and inactive, 51, 54, 108; is created, 20-22, 54; fourfold consideration of, 98-100, 102; is not a gift, 32; of this life and of heaven, 56, 75, 79, 81-85, 89, 97, 99-100, 103-104; need for, 25; and the virtues, 28-32, 35-39, 42, 46-49, 51-52, 55-56, 81, 106, 108

Chenu, M.-D., 2, 3, 5, 110

Citizen, duties of, 29

Command, and charity, 49

Commandment, of charity, 65

Contraries, cannot exist together, 67-68; and virtue, 108-109

Counsel: of charity, 69-70, 87, 90; of poverty, 87-88, 90; and precept, 66-69, 87, 92; of virginity, 87, 90

Creature: likeness to God, 23; is loved by God, 25; is vanity, 18, 23

Deeds, of love, 75

Definition, of charity, 21-22

Destrez, J., 2, 110

Difference, and genus and species, 97

Dionysius, 51, 74, 88, 95, 96, 110

Effect, of love, 75, 79

End: of charity, 48, 53; and final causality, 96; man's ultimate, 24; and object, 35-36; principal and secondary, 89-90; and virtue, 48; and will, 21

Enemies: hate of, 69-71; love of, 66, 68-73, 90

Enjoyment: and charity, 22; and the fruits, 27, 31.

Eschmann, I. T., 2, 111

Exemplar: and charity, 33-34, 37, 60; the First, 103

Faith: and charity, 38-39, 106; is in the cognitive power, 34; and God, 26; as an infused habit, 109; object of, 36, 52, 56, 74, 77, 109; order in, 74; is a special light, 34, 38

Fear: and charity, 82, 84; is a gift, 28; and love, 28

Fitzpatrick, M., 3, 111

Form: and charity, 56; confers being and species, 33, 35-36; end of the generation of a thing, 39; included in definition, 33; and manner, 23; and matter, 99; and perfect agent, 24; of virtue, 33-34, 38

Formal notion: of charity, 48; of love, 42-43

Friendship: is a certain equality, 27; of God and neighbor, 41; love of, 27, 44-45, 64, 73; of man for God, 31; of man to angels, 59, 63; of man to man, 27, 31, 73, 78; meaning of, 67; natural, 61; nature of, 68; political, 61; is a sharing, 59, 64; and virtue, 31

Glorieux, P., 2, 3, 111

God: acts without a medium, 19; form subsisting essentially, 25; is giver of charity, 97, 107; gives forms to created things, 24; is love, 23, 58; love of, 40-44, 48, 52-54, 58, 61-64, 73, 74, 76-77, 81-85, 90-91, 94, 97-100, 102, 104; is loved through Himself, 25; loves all things which exist, 19, 58, 62; moves all things, 20-22; is object of charity, 31, 36, 39; is present to the soul, 19, 25; is Supreme Good, 19

Good: and charity, 23-24, 26, 28, 32, 43, 61, 75, 97, 103; common, 43; contrariety in, 96, 102-103; is in God, 62; The Highest, 103; love of, 28-29, 49; of man, 19, 28, 43, 101; is object of virtue, 46, 49; political, 28-29; and virtue, 28

Goodness: artistic, 28; and love, 84; political, 28-29

Grabmann, M., 2, 3, 111

Grace: is caused by God, 24; joins man to God, 26, 30; and nature, 24; prin-

[113]

Temperance: and the concupiscible appetite, 48-49; is difficult to preserve, 26

Tremblay, P., 3, 111

Truth: and being, 77-78; and charity, 24, 101; is the conformity of intellect and thing, 77; the First, 24, 103

Union, of love, 22, 30, 74, 78, 81, 84

Unity, in charity, 41-42, 44

Van Steenberghen, F., 3, 112

Virtue: St. Augustine's definition of, 37, 41; concerns what is difficult, 26, 30, 51; differences in, 41, 45; general and special, 46; generation and corruption of, 47, 49-50, 51; infused, 29; moral, 55; need for, 47, 49; political, 28-29

Voluntariness, and end, 35

Voluntary, proceeds from an intrinsic principle 21

Vow: and charity, 93; of chastity, 90-91; of obedience, 90-91; of poverty, 90-91

Walz, A., 2, 112

Wellmuth, J., 3, 111

Will: act of, 55, 96; and charity, 20, 57, 75, 105; is mistress of its acts, 81, 85; object of, 35; is subject of virtue, 49

William of St. Thierry, 51, 54, 106, 108, 112